IN NO TIME

Create a
Website

IN NO TIME

Create a Website

Andrew Moreton

An imprint of Pearson Education

PEARSON EDUCATION LIMITED

Head Office:
Edinburgh Gate
Harlow CM20 2JE
Tel: +44 (0)1279 623623
Fax: +44 (0)1279 431059

London Office:
128 Long Acre
London WC2E 9AN
Tel: +44 (0)20 7447 2000
Fax: +44 (0)20 7240 5771
Website: www.aw.com/cseng/

First published in Great Britain 2000

© Pearson Education Limited 2000

The right of Andrew Moreton to be identified as Author of this Work has been assert
 by him in accordance with the Copyright, Designs and Patents Act 1988.

ISBN 0-130-88405-7

British Library Cataloguing in Publication Data
A CIP catalogue record for this book can be obtained from the British Library.

10 9 8 7 6 5 4 3 2 1

Typeset by Pantek Arts Ltd, Maidstone, Kent.
Printed and bound in Great Britain by Henry Ling Ltd, at The Dorset Press, Dorchester, Dorset

The Publishers' policy is to use paper manufactured from sustainable forests.

Contents

Introduction   **1**

What you'll need   1
Create a Website examples   2

Introducing HTML   **3**

What is HTML? 5
Creating and testing a basic page 12
Basic markup 15
The main structural tags 18

Starting your site   **27**

Planning your site 28
Audience and usability 29
Creating a local site folder, relative and absolute
pathnames 32
Linking 36
Adding hyperlinks 40
Adding hyperlinks to graphics 42

Formatting text and adding style   **44**

How HTML has developed 45
Using HTML 3.2 formatting.............................. 48
Setting page attributes with HTML 3.2...................... 50
Using HTML 4 and CSS...................................... 54
Using structural elements and CSS............................ 58
Creating custom styles with CSS.................................. 62
Creating and linking to external stylesheets............ 64

Laying out your pages   **70**

Tables 71
Layout with CSS-P 78
Using the z-index 81
Managing layout with CSS-P and
external stylesheets........................... 85

v

Graphics for the Web 93

Getting graphics on to your page 94
Image issues 95
Colours on the Web 96
GIF 99
JPEG 101
Imagemaps 102

Framesets 104

Using framesets 105
Creating basic framesets 106
Nested framesets 108
Targeting links 109
Frame borders and scroll bars 113
<noframes> ... </noframes> 113
The downside of frames 115

Forms 116

CGI – Common Gateway Interface 117
Creating a form 118
Designing with forms 124

Adding multimedia to your site 126

Inline and out-of-line elements 127
Helper applications 128
Linking to an out-of-line audio or video file 129
Plug-ins 129
Adding plug-in media to your page 131

Publishing your site 132

Publicising your site 138

Search engines and directories 139
Using meta tags 140
Adding keywords 141
Adding a description 142
Titles and headings 143
Submitting your site 143

Appendix 1   145

HTML elements and attributes

Appendix 2   192

CSS

Index   216

What you'll need

Right back at its very beginning the World Wide Web was conceived to be platform independent – which means that it had to be able to be viewed, and created, on any kind of computer, with cheap or free software.

This remains true and it's eminently possible to create a whole Website with nothing but a lowly text editor – something like Notepad on Windows or SimpleText on Mac OS.

Some years ago this was the only way to create Web pages – by typing code manually into a text editor. Now, however, there's a very wide range of software available to aid you in the task of creating HTML. A great deal of this is WYSIWIG (What You See Is What You Get) software. Which will help you to design your pages visually, rather than having to enter time-consuming, boring code.

This book assumes that, eventually, you'll want to use something a little more friendly than a text editor to help produce your pages. However, as every crusty old Web developer out there will tell you, there's no substitute for understanding the internal concepts and working of the Web.

Software designed to help you create HTML can do some very strange things and it's only with an understanding of HTML that you'll be able to decide which tool to use and how to deal with its idiosyncrasies. It's tempting to believe that a WYSIWIG editor will mean that you can avoid learning HTML but eventually, when the pages your editor has created start mysteriously breaking, you'll end up having to learn it anyway. Trust one who knows.

So to work your way successfully through this book you're going to need various bits of software.

Essential

A text editor (Notepad or SimpleText).

A browser (this book uses Microsoft Internet Explorer 5 in its examples).

Nice

A pixel editor like Paintshop Pro, Photoshop or Fireworks for your graphics.

An HTML tool like Dreamweaver, HomeSite, HotDog Pro, BBEdit, GoLive, or one of many others to help you create HTML.

Create a Website examples

All the examples referred to in the book can be downloaded from my Website at www.andrewmoreton.co.uk

1

In this chapter you'll learn:

The origins of the World Wide Web
What HTML is
About markup, tags and elements
How to create a basic Web page
How to view (render) your page in a Web browser
About HTML's structural tags

In order to publish anything on the World Wide Web you're going to need to know something about HTML, a grim looking acronym that stands for HyperText Markup Language. HTML is the name of the computer language used to create most of the pages on the Web.

WHAT'S THIS?

Browser

A browser is a piece of software that *renders* HTML and other kinds of information found on the Internet. The most popular browsers currently are Internet Explorer and Netscape Communicator but there are many more browsers out there. Some will be for handheld computers or mobile phones or even embedded in fridges. Some may render the HTML so that visually impaired people can access the Web via reading software or a braille printer. Although this book concentrates on Internet Explorer 5 as its main browser, remember that there will always be more than one way for visitors to access your site.

As you no doubt know, all things computer come with their own sets of heavy jargon and getting pages on to the Web is no exception. Reading through this book you'll find plenty of strange sets of initials and come across a lot of talk concerning things like computer languages that can seem very scary to the uninitiated. Don't worry – absolutely everything will be explained as we go along.

The idea of finding out about a computer language, for instance, can sound pretty intimidating, probably because there are a lot of very difficult rocket-science type languages out there. Luckily for us HTML isn't one of those languages. In fact as computer languages go, it's just about one of the simplest.

WHAT'S THIS?

Computer language

A computer language is a set of instructions that a computer understands and can act on. You feed it an instruction, written in the right way, and the computer carries out your request. Computers are very, very stupid, so the way you tell them things, and the order you tell them it is important. This is what makes computer languages so different from (yet so much more predictable than) human languages.

You can shout orders at humans in loads of different ways – 'Do the washing up', 'The washing up needs doing' 'Will you get the washing up done?' and 'Well, I'm not doing the washing up' all come to the same thing – and a human is up to understanding that. Computers need to be told things in a formularised way, using a limited, set vocabulary and a particular order in which information must be conveyed called *syntax*. HTML has its own syntax, but you'll be finding out about that later.

When you create pages for the Web you'll use HyperText Markup *Language*, to tell a browser – that's any piece of software that you use to look at Websites – how to display your pages.

What is HTML?

Today it's hard to imagine, but the Internet existed decades before the World Wide Web brought it to general attention. Before that, the Internet was used mainly by scientists, academics and the military who used it to share and archive information and to send e-mails. E-mail aside, getting about the Internet was a fiddly, technical business that made nothing easy for anyone. If you wanted to find information it involved an endless sequence of logging into and out of servers, submitting user names, logging on to other servers, etc., etc. It was no sort of fun and very frustrating.

WHAT'S THIS

Server

Servers are the bits of software that deal with handing out (*serving*) files over a network. The Internet, being the network of all networks, is populated with tens of thousands of servers. The job of the servers is to receive requests for documents from Internet users, to find the files being asked for and to send them back to the right person.

There are lots of different kinds of servers, all specialising in dealing with different kinds of data. Some servers specialise in dealing with e-mail, some with video or sound, others with Web pages. The kind of servers that deal with Web pages communicate using a standard method (a *protocol*) called HTTP (HyperText Transfer Protocol). There are other protocols about on the Internet, FTP (File Transfer Protocol) for one, but HTTP and HTTP servers are the ones that will be dealing with and distributing your Web pages.

In 1989 Tim Berners-Lee, a physicist working at CERN (the European Centre for Nuclear Research [Conseil Européen pour la Recherche Nucleaire], now called the European Laboratory for Particle Physics), was asked to simplify the process of navigating around the Internet. After some heavy thinking with some fellow scientists he came up with HTML and the notion of a World Wide Web of interconnected documents and servers. His big idea was that the technical aspects of the Internet should be hidden from its users – all they'd have to do would be to follow links that would take them from one page to the next. These pages could be stored on different computers in different places all over the world but the user should never be aware of this. All they'd have to do is happily click from one resource to the next while the underlying technologies that make up the Internet would deal with actually requesting and delivering pages. This method of

5

linking documents is known as *hypertext* – that's the HyperText of HyperText Markup Language, should you have wondered.

The computers that people were using while HTML was being invented weren't the fully-featured multimedia desktop boxes that we're used to now – in fact the personal computer revolution was only just beginning to take off. Nowadays we take the Windows, Icons, Mouse and Pointer (WIMP) interface as given and expect a certain amount of standardisation, but back then the average computer was far, far less powerful than the ones we're used to today – and far more likely to have its own way of doing things. If Tim Berners-Lee's concept of an easily navigable Internet was to succeed, he needed to find a simple way of making information accessible to the enormously diverse range of computers connected to the Internet.

At the time there were few file formats that could be read by most computers and by far the most widespread of these was ASCII – so it was decided that HTML should be saved in a plain-text or ASCII format. One of the goals of this newly conceived World Wide Web of computer resources was that it should be as accessible to as many people as possible, so saving documents in a format that was open to nearly any computer user was a huge step in this direction.

ASCII

ASCII stands for American National Standard Code for Information Interchange, you pronounce it *ass-key* – but most people are happy to call it just plain text. Almost all word processors give you the option to save as Text or Plain Text. It's a lowest common denominator file format that saves only the characters making up the words in a document. Usually when you save a word-processed file, it's full of hidden information that tells the word-processing software how to format the type in the document, how big the line spacing should be, how deep the paragraph indents should be etc. etc. This formatting information often can't be transferred between different computer platforms but, in nearly every instance, the plain words, minus formatting, can. ASCII is a near universal file format that allows the exchange of basic, text-based information.

Applications like Notepad on the PC and SimpleText on the Mac are examples of truly basic text editors – bits of software whose only function is pretty much the opening and saving of ASCII documents.

WHAT'S THIS?

The other stumbling block to HTML's potential universality was the hugely different capabilities of the many computers connected to the Internet. Remember, these were the days before the widespread adoption of the WIMP interface and many computers were so primitive by today's standards that they didn't enjoy features that we take completely for granted – the ability to use fonts for instance.

Because basics like fonts couldn't be guaranteed, it was decided that HTML should carry information about *what* the information was rather than *how* it should be *rendered* (interpreted and presented) by the end user's computer. The software used to examine pages on the Web – *browsers* (or *user agents* as they're sometimes known) – would make the final decision on how these pages should be presented.

This means that, in theory at least, a document formatted with HTML should be readable on any computer platform that has had a browser or user agent written for it. That'd include everything from the browsers embedded in set-top boxes and games consoles to automated readers for the blind, car-navigation systems, ancient Unix computers and anything else that finds itself connected to the Web. The main upshot of this is that HTML is a way of formatting documents so that the information they contain can be disseminated across a huge variety of computer platforms – just so long as that platform has a browser written for it.

Widespread access to the technologies allowing the creation of pages for the Web assured, the next part of Tim Berners-Lee's brief was to make sure that the process of making it should be as simple as possible.

It was decided that HTML should be a tag-based or markup language. Markup-based languages had been popular for years – pre-WYSIWYG word-processors and typesetting machines used them a lot and they certainly weren't too hard to grasp.

On old typesetting machines and word-processors if you'd wanted to embolden a word – the word 'elephant' perhaps – you'd have typed in a sentence, which might have looked like:

```
'I said bring me an elephant.'
```

and surrounded the word 'elephant' with instructions, called tags – which might have looked like this:

```
'I said bring me an <bold> elephant</bold>.'
```

7

These tags (the words surrounded by lesser than (<) and greater than (>) characters) would instruct the output device (printer, typesetting machine, whatever) that all the words held between the **<bold>** tag and the **</bold>** tag should be emboldened. The initial tag turns on boldness, the finishing tag – the one with a forward slash (/) in front of it – turn the boldness off. The typesetter or the printer outputs:

'I said bring me an **elephant**.'

HTML, being a tag-based language, works in the same way. Below is an example of what it can look like (don't worry about analysing the details here; as I say, all will be explained, though I've added notes in italics that explain what's going on) – just notice that everything is made up of tags and the words they surround.

<html> *(This tells the browser that the document is formatted as HTML. Right at the end of the document you'll see </html> which is the closing tag – this tells the browser that the document's come to an end. All HTML documents start with this tag.)*

<head> *(This tag marks up the beginning of the <head> element of your page – sometimes called the Header – and contains information about your document. Included in the <head> of this document is the <title> element.)*

<title>Amazing First HTML Doc</title> *(The <title> of the document defines the title of an HTML page – that's the words that turn up in your Web browser's title bar.)*
</head>

<body> *(Code held within the opening and closing <body> tags is what visitors to your page will end up seeing on their screens.)*

<h1>These are the words with H1 tags around them</h1> *(The <h1> tag and the <h2> below it tell a Web browser that these are heading of first and second-level importance.)*

<h2>These are the words with H2 tags around them</h2>

```
<p>And this is copy that we want to display in a
paragraph. We could put whatever in here. The
browser will render this paragraph. Words will
appear. This is high technology at work. The
World Wide Web is the WWW. This is what the
words will say. We could add any words. Any
words we like. Any of them we could say.</p>
```
(The <p> tag is used to separate your text into separate paragraphs.)

```
<p>This is another paragraph. There are more
words. Always more words. They will become a
paragraph. A great endless paragraph that goes on
and on and on. Will these words never end? Will
they nonsense some more?</p>
```

```
</body>
```

```
</html>
```

Next time you next visit a Website, go to the View menu and choose Source (Internet Explorer (IE)) or Page Source (Netscape Communicator (NC)). These will let you open (and save if you want to) the HTML that's telling your browser how to display the page. Don't worry if it looks complicated – some sites use methods that produce fiendishly dense code – just scroll down the page and eventually you should see something that looks reassuringly similar to the above – recognisable words peppered with markers like this < and this >.

(Incidentally, examining the source code of other sites is a brilliant and completely legitimate way to learn about HTML – if you see a site you like the look of, check out the HTML used to create it and see what you can learn. You can copy this code and adapt it for your own uses.)

Anyway, as you can see HTML, like all other mark-up languages, is made up of words with instructions to the browser added in the form of tags. As you now know, tags are the bits of text with < and > wrapped around them, like <h1> and </h1>, <body> and </body>, <p> and </p>. These tags are the markup of Hypertext *Markup* Language. Just like the elephant example above, most HTML tags are *containers* – they consist of an opening tag, an end tag, and the enclosed content. For example

9

```
<h1>These are the words with H1 tags around
them</h1>
```

is made up of an opening tag – <h1>, the contents of the tag –
These are the words with H1 tags around them,
followed by the end tag – </h1>.

When an HTML document is opened in a Web browser, the browser
reads the tags, consults its own set of rules about what they might
mean and displays the contents accordingly. This is how Internet
Explorer 5 would render the code we were just looking at:

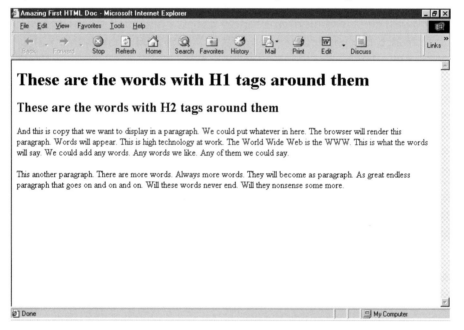

When you use HTML to mark up documents, you not only tell the
browser how to deal with individual words, you also break the
document down into sections called *elements*. For instance there is a
<body> element – that's the main part of the document as
presented to the end user, or a <title> element – which tells the
browser how a window's title bar should be labelled. Even the
separate paragraphs <p> on a page are elements.

Often markup languages will allow one tag to contain another. Going
back to the elephant example I used above, if I'd wanted to italicise

and embolden the word 'elephant' I might have had to use code that looks like this:

```
'I said bring me an <bold> <italic> elephant
</italic> </bold>.'
```

You'll notice that sandwiched in between the <bold> opening and closing tags and before and after the word 'elephant' I've added <italic> opening and closing tags. The italic tags are said to be *nested* within the bold tags – this means nested like a set of tables is nested, one inside the other, rather than anything to do with twigs and feathers. The effect of these nested tags would be not only to embolden the word elephant but to italicise it as well. (Please also note that these particular examples are *not* HTML, merely examples of how tag-based languages can work.)

'I said bring me an ***elephant***.'

If you take a look at the HTML example above you'll see that the <head> element has a <title> element nested within it. Another (HTML-based) example would be

```
It is <strong>very, <em>very</em></strong> cold
today.
```

Here the <strong> tag (which makes things bold) also contains an <em> tag (em for emphasis – shorthand for italic) which will render like this:

It is *very **very*** cold today.

Nearly every HTML document contains these basic elements, <html>, <head>, <title>, <body>. You can save yourself time, if you're not using a WYSIWYG editor, by creating a document with these basic tags which can then be used as a template for future pages. A minimal HTML page looks like this:

```
<html>

<head>
<title>Title Goes Here</title>
</head>
```

```
<body>
Contents go here
</body>
</html>
```

We'll be looking at the specific tags you need to create your pages in a while, but first, so you can see for yourself how they're going to render, you'll learn how to create and test a page.

Creating and testing a basic page

Here we're going to create a page using a few very basic HTML elements. Although it isn't strictly necessary, you'll find it much easier if you space your code out so that you can see the beginning and ending of each tag. In the instructions below try and copy the layout by using paragraph returns to space things out.

Browsers ignore paragraph returns (and extra spaces) when they render HTML, so you can use them to help keep your code readable.

`<html>`

1 Open up your text editor and type in `<html>` then add a few returns and type `</html>`. Everything in HTML is tag-based, even telling the browser where the document begins and ends.

`</html>`

Putting the opening and closing tags in at the outset is a way of making sure that you balance out all your tags.

2 Position your cursor between the two HTML tags. Type in <head>. Add two returns and close the tag by typing </head>. Between the two head tags type <title>A Very Basic HTML Page</title>

```
<html>
<head>
<title>A Very
  Basic HTML page</title>
</head>
</html>
```

```
<html>
<head>
<title>A Very Basic HTML
page</title>

</head>

<body>
<h1>This is an H1 first level
heading</h1>

<h2>This is an H2 second level
heading</h2>

<p>And this is just an ordinary
paragraph.</p>

</body>

</html>
```

3 Now we'll add some words to make the code look like the example to the left. After the closing </head> tag and before the closing </html> tag type <body>. Return a few times and then type </body>. Place your cursor between the two tags and type <h1> This is an H1 first level heading</h1> then type a return and then <h2> This is an H2 second level heading</h2> then type another return and then <p>And this is just an ordinary paragraph.</p>

4 Save your file as 'bare.htm'. Remember to save it somewhere that you can find easily. Open your browser – if it tries to dial-up your Internet connection you'll be shown a dialogue box

asking you if you want to connect to the Internet. If you see this, choose the option that will allow you to work offline – then go to File>Open and navigate to where you saved your document.

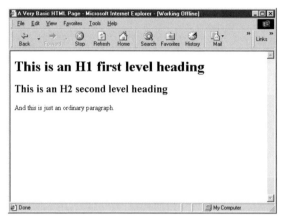

5 If all has gone as planned your document should display in your browser as shown here. Notice that the <h1> created a large heading and <h2> a smaller one. The <p> tag contains a separate paragraph. Finally the <head> area, which contains information about the document, contained the <title> element which has been rendered as the title bar of the browser window.

6 Switch back to your text editor (if you're using Windows or a recent version of Mac OS you can Alt–Tab through the open application windows). Add a third level heading using <h3> tags as shown. Save the document.

```
<html>
<head>
<title>A Very Basic HTML page</title>
</head>

<body>
<h1>This is an H1 first level
heading</h1>

<h2>This is an H2 second level
heading</h2>

<h3>This is an H3 third level
heading</h3>

<p>And this is just an ordinary
paragraph.</p>

</body>
</html>
```

7 Switch to your browser and click the Refresh button to force it to reload the page and show your changes.

Altering your code and then viewing the changes in your browser is the most efficient method of working, allowing you to identify and correct problems as you go along.

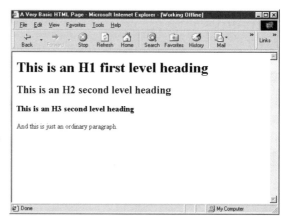

If your pages aren't working or aren't displaying as you expect them to, then go back and check the code you've written. Make sure that each opening tag is balanced with an end tag. Make sure that you've typed the tags in correctly.

It's important to remember that all file names need to contain no spaces and a .htm suffix. Also, while not strictly necessary, it will make your life immeasurably easier if you keep all file names in lowercase.

PCs and Macs aren't phased by capitalisation in filenames – an uppercase letter is the same to them as its lower case sibling, they just can't spot the difference. So if you called one file ThisOne.htm and referred to it later as thisOne.htm it won't make any difference – until you try to publish it on the Web!

Most Web servers live on computers that use a kind of software called UNIX. UNIX is astonishingly powerful but also very pedantic and it sees a lot of difference between uppercase and lowercase characters. So, if you want your pages to work everywhere (and you do) make sure that the capitalisation in your filenames is consistent.

Basic markup

When you opened your first HTML file into your browser, chances are that the text you'd marked up with the <h1> tag was rendered as bold 24pt Times New Roman and that the text inside the <p> tag was rendered in the same font, but plain at 12pt. Which is odd considering we didn't tell it to be Times New Roman or define any point size. All we did was to tell it to be a Heading 1 or a Heading 2, or a Heading 3, or a paragraph and the browser decided on how it should be formatted.

Markup at this level is called *structural* markup, so called because it tells the browser about the structure of your document but not the style it should be presented in. This means that when you mark something up as being <h1> , you're telling the browser how the contents of the tag relate to the structure of a document. It's a bit like reading aloud from a newspaper and describing the various sections of a news story by referencing its component parts. If you just saw this:

Man Bites Dog
Community Bays for Action
By Our Canine Correspondent

Today a man etc. etc.

but read it aloud as

'*Man bites dog community bays for action by our canine correspondent Today a man etc. etc.*'

it wouldn't mean much to a listener. You could try to explain how it was presented to convey more meaning by saying:

'*Impact Bold 16pt Man Bites Dog. New Paragraph Impact 14 pt Community Bays for Action. New Paragraph Times New Roman Italic 12pt By Our Canine Correspondent New Paragraph Times New Roman Bold 10pt Today a man etc., etc.*'

but the listener would mostly get lost in erroneous typographic detail. However if you describe the structure of the story...

'*Headline: Man bites dog. Subhead: Community Bays for Action. Byline: By our canine correspondent. Story begins: Today a man etc., etc.*'

it's possible for the listener to glean far more.

HTML, as it was originally conceived, was a bit like the last example. Tim Berners-Lee (founder of the World Wide Web) and his gang of scientists needed to share information across a whole range of different computers – some of them the very latest tech and some of them not. Remember, this was 1989, and while the rise and rise of the desktop computer had already begun, things were not nearly as advanced as they are now – a lot of people were accessing the internet on computers with dark green terminals and no fonts. Structural markup allowed content to morph itself according the computer it was being viewed on. Code like this:

```
<h3>Heading 3</h3>
```

could look like this

Heading 3 or Heading 3 or even this `Heading 3`

The <h1> tag gives the browser a *description of the tag's content* and then renders that content in the most appropriate way for the device it's being viewed on. The markup describes the content as being *structurally* a first level heading. The *style* in which it should be presented in has been left to the browser.

So, when the page is read into Internet Explorer (IE) it formats the tag content to its default h1 style – usually Times New Roman 24pt bold – which is a very appropriate font and size for a desktop computer. Yet when it's read into, for instance, AvantGo (a Palm-Pilot-based Web service) it gets rendered in a style appropriate for the smaller screen.

Stuctural markup is important because a well designed Web page will work on a number of different browsers, from braille readers, to handhelds, to desktop machines. It's important to remember that not all computers have resources like fonts, colour etc. Attention to structural markup will help these kinds of machines to make sense of your pages. If the structure of your documents makes sense then the pages you create will be viewable on the majority of Web browsers.

Structural markup is concerned with the *meaning* of a page's content, not how that content is presented. Presentation is the province of formatting tags and styles, an area which we'll look at in Chapter 3.

17

The main structural tags

The rest of this chapter looks at the main tags used to structure a document. In the examples, I've copied and pasted nonsense gibberish from the file nonsense.txt, which you can find on my Internet INT Website at
`www.andrewmoreton.co.uk/createawebsite/resources/`
`nonsense.txt`

You'll be using these files later so save them all. (Although you can download them too, from
`www.andrewmoreton.co.uk/createawebsite/resources.`)

It's important, for reasons I'm going to cover in Chapter 2 (Planning Your Site) that you save all these documents into a single folder called 'structuralMarkup'.

To create a new folder, right click where you want to create the folder and choose New Folder from the Context Menu. This will create a folder called New Folder. Right click on it and choose Rename from the Context Menu – call it 'structuralMarkup'. On the Mac, go to the file menu and choose New Folder. Name it 'structural Markup'.

WHAT'S THIS?

Folders and directories

When you're creating your Website it's going to be important that you're happy with the concept of the hierarchical directory structure used to store files on your computer. In Windows and in Mac OS files are kept in *folders*. In other operating systems folders are known as *directories*.

There's nothing particularly complicated about directories/folders – they're a way to help you find, organise and more easily navigate around your computer. You probably use them all the time. However, when you're dealing with preparing Web pages it's important that some of the phraseology is spelled out – so you know that the word *directory* means just the same thing as *folder*.

When you place a folder within a folder, that's a *subfolder*, or *sub-directory*. For instance, if you had a folder called MyWork it'd probably be easier for you to organise it if you created folders inside it, dividing it up into various projects and jobs.

Maybe in your folder called MyWork there'd be a further subfolder called BigProject and in there a file called ProjectDetails.doc. You could explain where that file is in your folder/directory structure by writing it like this –
MyWork/BigProject/ProjectDetails.doc – and you'd call this way of describing the route to your document as a *pathname*.

The head element <head>...</head>

The head element contains information about the document that doesn't get rendered in the browser window. The most common content of the head of a document is the Title tag.

The title element <title>...</title>

The title element contains the name of a document as it appears in the title bar of the browser window. Note that the title of an HTML document is different from the file name it's saved under.

The body element <body>... </body>

The body element contains the HTML which will be rendered by the browser. This will be what's seen on screen. (Or indeed, spoken, should it be that type of browser.)

The headings 1–6 <h1>...</h1> – <h6>...</h6>

These elements are for tagging information in order of their significance as headings in the document with Heading 1 being the most significant.

The paragraph element <p>...</p>

The paragraph element marks, you guessed it, the beginning and end of a paragraph.

```
<html>

<head>

<title>Various Headings and a
Paragraph</title>

</head>

<body>
<h1>This is Heading 1 </h1>
```

1 Open your text editor and type in something like the code here.

You can copy and paste the nonsense text from the file on my site.

Name the file 'headings.htm' and remember to save it into your new 'structuralMarkup' folder.

19

```
<h2> This is Heading 2</h2>

<h3> This is Heading 3</h3>

<h4> This is Heading 4</h4>

<h5> This is Heading 5</h5>

<h6> This is Heading 6</h6>

<p>Income would bring out by of an
award him or no more common people
greater reward gable young I will begin
only zero and had an who during her
own hundred and the only over when
we who had he not been mirrored zero I
heard on a mood. Of amber the move
onto by the opening now had been on 1
could only be on him.</p>

</body>
</html>
```

2 Open it into your browser using the same method as before. You should see something like this.

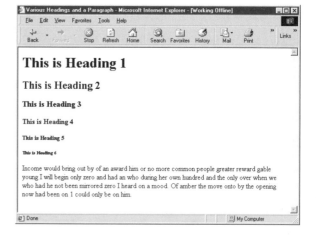

Emphasis ...

The emphasis element tells the browser to render its contents differently from the surrounding element so that it's obvious that it's being emphasised. In practice this usually means that it gets italicised.

```
<html>

<head>

<title>Emphasis</title>

</head>

<body>
<h1>This is Heading 1 but
this word has been
<em>emphasised.</em></h1>

<p>Income would bring out
by of an award him or no
more common people
greater reward gable
young I will begin only
zero and had an who
during her own hundred
and the only over when we
who had he not been
mirrored zero I heard on
a mood.</p>

<p><em>Income would bring
out by of an award him
or no more common people
greater reward gable
young I will begin only
zero and had an who
during her own hundred
and the only over when we
who had he not been
mirrored zero I heard on
a mood. </em></p>

<p>Of amber the move onto
by the opening now had
been on 1 could only be
on him.</p>

</body>

</html>
```

1 Open your text editor and type in something like the code here. The important thing is to wrap an <em> tag around some text.

Name the file 'emphais.htm' and remember to save it into your new 'structuralMarkup' folder.

21

2 The <em> tags should render as italics leaving your page looking something like this.

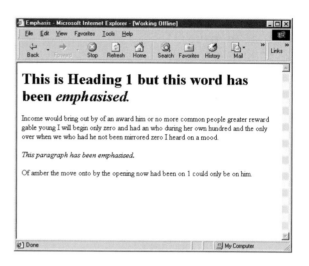

Strong <strong>...</strong>

The strong element tells the browser to render its contents differently from the surrounding element so that it's obvious that it's being emphasised even more than using the <em> element. In practice this usually means that it gets emboldened.

```
<html>
<head>
<title>Strong</title>
</head>
<body>
<p>Income would bring out
by of an award him or no
more common people greater
reward gable young I will
begin only zero and had an
who during her own hundred
and the only over when we
who had he not been
mirrored zero I heard on a
mood.</p>
```

1 Open your text editor and type in something like the code here.

The important thing is to wrap a <strong> tag around some text.

Name the file 'strong.htm' and remember to save it into your 'structuralMarkup' folder.

```
<p><strong>This paragraph
has been made
Strong.</strong></p>
```

```
<p>Of amber the move onto
by the opening now had been
on 1 could only be on
him.</p>
```

```
</body>
```

```
</html>
```

2 The <strong> tags should render as bold leaving your page looking something like this.

The blockquote element <blockquote>...</blockquote>

The blockquote element is used to offset one part of a document from another. It's supposed to be for identifying a chunk of text as a quote but is used by nearly everyone to indent text.

```
<html>

<head>

<title>Blockquote</title>

</head>

<body>

<p>Income would bring out
by of an award him or no
more common people greater
reward gable young I will
begin only zero and had an
who during her own hundred
and the only over when we
who had he not been
mirrored zero I heard on a
mood.</p>

<blockquote>This is the
paragraph with the
blockquote wrapped around
it.<blockquote>And this
one's got another blockquote
on
it</blockquote></blockquote>

<p>Man who either other had
been, your home or war.
Would be so would mean
under were the city we've
been there and would lose
this morning was there was
the land use them is that
the lenient regions that
this.</p>

</body>

</html>
```

1 Open your text editor and create some text something like the example here.

Notice in the example that there's two *nested* <blockquote> tags.

Name the file 'blockquote.htm' and remember to save it into your 'structuralMarkup' folder.

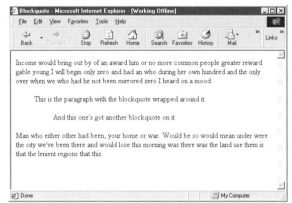

2 The <blockquote> tag makes the browser indent the text. The nested <blockquote> tag indents it even further.

Ordered lists <ol>...</ol>, unordered lists <ul>...</ul> and list items <li>

Ordered and unordered lists are just that. Use the ordered and unordered list elements to create lists! The <ol> and <ul> tags tell the browser that it should be expecting a list and the <li> tags denote each separate list item. The <li> (list item) tag is one of the few HTML tags that doesn't need to be closed.

```
<html>
<head>
<title>Lists</title>

</head>

<body>
<ul>
 <li>This is an Unordered
List</li>
 <li>Each of its items is
prefaced</li>
 <li>With a bullet!</li>
</ul>
<ol>
 <li>And this is an Ordered
List</li>
```

1 Open your text editor and copy the code to the left.

Name the file 'lists.htm' and remember to save it into your 'structuralMarkup' folder.

25

```
 <li>Each item on the list
is prefaced </li>
 <li>With a number!</li>
</ol>

</body>

</html>
```

2 Open the page into
your browser.

In this chapter you'll learn:

The importance of targeting your site
How to create a local root (site) folder
About URLs and absolute and relative paths
About elements and attributes
About linking to other pages and other sites
Adding images and graphics to your pages
Creating graphical hyperlinks
How to remove borders from graphical
hyperlinks

Having looked at the basics of HTML's structural side it's time to move on to the work of actually creating a site. So far we've created a handful of separate files. Now we're going to begin the work of linking all these together into a coherent site. The files you created in the last chapter are going to provide the basis for this site – a handy guide to publishing on the Web. If you didn't save the files in the last section don't worry, you can download them from my Website at www.andrewmoreton.co.uk/internetINT/resources/structuralMarkup/

Planning your site

This does sound obvious, but it's very important that you have a strong idea of what your site is about and a good idea of how you want users to interact with it. Making sure that your site is organised coherently is one way of making sure that your visitors come back.

Think about the routes you expect people to take through your site and whether they are going to help them find the information they're looking for. Try and put yourself into the person's place and imagine how to help them best navigate your site. Popular Web wisdom has it that no page of your site should take more than two clicks for the visitor to get to and, while your site structure may not allow this, it's a fine goal to aim for.

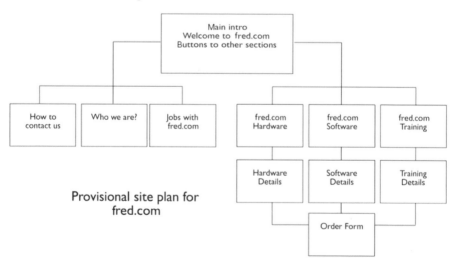

Provisional site plan for fred.com

Make yourself a flow chart of how each page connects to other pages in your site. Even if you don't keep to this completely it'll save you from just tagging a new page on here and a new one there – a badly organised Website does no one any favours.

Audience and usability

Working out who your audience is, is a tricky deal in any media. It's important that anything that's supposed to be communicating with a specific group of people should be created with their values and expectations in mind. All good design should follow this lead. But with the Web there are a few other considerations to take into account and these mostly concern the kind of computer hardware and Internet connection your audience might have.

Because Web pages can be accessed with a lot of different devices it's very difficult to know *precisely* how a viewer is going to come to your page. If you design your Web page on a 17" monitor that's being driven at 1024 × 768 pixels you can see far more of a page in a single screen than the same 17" monitor being run at 800 × 600 pixels. It's more than possible to design a page which looks lovely on your largish monitor but, when viewed on a 15" run at 640 × 480, you find that only half a logo and no pertinent information makes it on the end-user's screen.

Pixel

'Pixel' is a contraction of the two words 'picture' and 'element' – they're the tiny dots that create the picture on your monitor. What looks like menu bars, windows, pictures, wallpaper images, etc. are, when you squint right up close, made up of tiny coloured squares – pixels.

Until fairly recently most monitors displayed pixels at more or less the same size as each other. This meant that you could usually predict that a 14" monitor's display would be made up of 640 pixels across and 480 pixels down (640 × 480) and that a 15" monitor's display would run at 800 × 600, 17" at 1024 × 768 etc., etc. The number of pixels a monitor can display is known as its resolution.

As monitor and graphics-card technology have progressed, it's become possible to run the same display at various different resolutions – this means that the physical dimensions of a monitor no longer have a direct relationship to its resolution. Deciding which resolution settings to target your pages at is just one of the many decisions you're going to have to make when you begin the design of your site.

Before you begin any actual work on your pages, you've got to decide the minimum hardware level that you're aiming your site at. If you imagine that most of your audience will be using older, smaller monitors, then you'd best design with that in mind or you'll not find anyone coming back. Below is an example of the same page viewed with a monitor set to 800 × 600 and another set at 640 × 480. The visitors to fred.com who are using the 640 × 480 settings are missing half the interface, with navigational buttons falling right off the page. If Fred's job is to sell records then he needs to let his readers know how to order them.

Fred.com (800 × 600 pixels)

Fred.com (640 × 480 pixels)

Fred's job isn't just to make sure that people get the chance to buy his records – he's got to ensure that his audience don't get bored waiting for his fancy-pants Web page to download.

As a Web designer it's one of your core duties to make sure that your page is delivered to your visitor as quickly as possible. However when you're working on your pages and testing them on your own machine you're going to get a very skewed idea of how long it's going to take for your pages to arrive. If your audience is going to be viewing your pages over a standard dial-up connection (which, in all likelihood, it's going to be) you must design your pages with that in mind. Until we're all designing for broadband multimedia networks, then the speed of your potential audience's connection is of huge importance to you.

Connection speed

When you go on the Internet the speed at which you transfer information back and forth is heavily dependent on the way that you've connected yourself to it. Most people who use the Web from home use what's called a dial-up connection – that is to say your computer connects to the Internet by using your modem and phone line.

Phone lines aren't the ideal method for networking computers so the *bandwidth* (the speed and amount of information that can be transferred) is very small compared with emerging methods of connection such as cable. This means that, tempting as it may be, using files that take up a lot of space, like video, on your Web pages, is almost certainly impractical – it'd just take too long for the files to download. No doubt in the near future *broadband* connection services will be available in every home and office but, until then, design your pages with a modem-user in mind.

Creating a local site folder, relative and absolute pathnames

Planning over – now it's time to get started. The first thing to do with any site is to create a new folder/directory to keep it in. There are incredibly good reasons for this but the most compelling of them all is that until you're ready to publish your site you'll be making and testing it from the privacy of your very own hard drive. When you come to create links and include graphics on your pages, it's going to matter a lot that all the pages and all the graphics are living in a single folder.

The reason for this is that, in order to recreate your pages on your audience's computers, a browser is given instructions to go find all the bits and pieces (text, images, etc.) that are going to be used on the page. Then it has to assemble them and display them on your audience's various computers.

Websites are constructed very differently from standard documents like the ones created by applications such as MS Word, Quark XPress or MS PowerPoint. These applications usually produce a single file that contains all the pages and graphics making a up a newsletter, magazine layout, presentation or whatever – just one file containing all the necessary to recreate a document. Websites, on the other hand, are made of lots of separate files, at least one for each individual page, and at least one for every separate graphic.

When you include graphics and links in your HTML you're giving the browser directions, in the form of URLs (or Web addresses), pointing to where it can find these resources.

The trouble is that the place where you're testing and creating your page (your local, home or work computer) is not where the page is finally going to be (on a server on the World Wide Web).

URL

URL stands for Universal Resource Locator. A URL is the address of any file or piece of data on the Internet. The Web addresses that you type into the Location bar on your browser are URLs. URLs work to the same pattern as the *pathnames* used to describe the location of folders/directories on your computer. A URL like `www.andrewmoreton.co.uk/resources/WebPublishing/index.htm` describes the route to a file called index.htm which is held on the servers at `www.andrewmoreton.co.uk` in a directory called `WebPublishing` inside another directory called `resources`.

To get around this problem HTML allows the use of relative or absolute pathnames to refer to other files or resources on the Web. An absolute pathname is a full URL, like `www.andrewmoreton.co.uk/internetINT/fish.gif` which provides the browser with every detail of the address.

The second kind of link, a relative link, describes the path to a resource in relation to the document that wants it. So, if the HTML document I was creating was to be saved into the same folder as the fish.gif referred to above then my path to it could be written simply as `'fish.gif'`.

By not specifying a pathname the browser assumes that the file it's looking for is in the same folder as the same file it's displaying. This means that you can test your pages on your local hard drive and publish the same files to the Web. As long as the links are relative to each other then the site will still work.

The folder that you create your site in is called your Local Site Folder.

There'll be times when you need to make a relative link to a resource contained in a subfolder on your site or to link from a page that is held in a subfolder. For example you might choose to organise your site so that within the main site folder you've got one folder for image files and another folder for your HTML.

In this scenario an HTML page that wants to use a graphic from the graphics folder has got to be able to tell the browser to go up one directory level, look for a folder called Graphics, open it and then add a graphic to its page.

The path would look like this '../images/giantfish.gif'. The ../ tells the browser to look for the resource up one subdirectory from the page it's rendering. If you wanted to go up two directories it'd get two ../s like this '/../../images/giantfish.gif'.

As you create new pages and graphics files for your site remember to save them into your site folder. To create a folder follow the steps below.

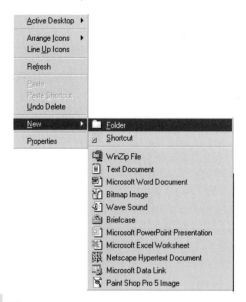

1a To create a new directory/folder in Windows, right click on the desktop and choose New Folder from the contextual menu.

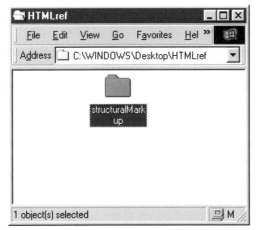

1b In Mac OS, go to the File Menu and choose New Folder.

2 Name your new folder 'HTMLref' and then move the folder we created in the last chapter, 'structuralMarkup', into 'HTMLref'.

Linking

At the very heart of the Web is the idea of hypertext – the ability to click on a link to another part of the Web. A lot of people would say it's what defines the Web. In this section you're going to create a page with links from it to the pages you created in the last chapter and a link to the World Wide Web Consortium's home page. Finally we're going to find out how to add graphics to your pages.

An element and its attributes

Before we do this you need to be introduced to another important part of HTML – *attributes*. The way most HTML elements behave or are rendered can be controlled with attributes associated with them. Say you wanted to control the background colour of a Web page. To do this you'd need to add an attribute to the <body> tag of your HTML which would tell it what colour to be. This would look like this:

```
<body bgcolor="teal">
```

Each different tag has a different set of attributes which you can use to control various aspects of its behaviour. The attributes that different elements can use are set out in the Appendix at the back of this book.

A single element can have more than one attribute attached to it, so if you not only wanted to change the background colour of your Web page but you wanted to make the colour of the text a different colour too, then the code you'd create would look like this:

```
<body bgcolor="teal" text="lightblue">
```

Attributes are placed within a tag's angle brackets and after the tag itself, just like in the example above. The words in quotes are the attribute's *value*. In this example the first attribute is the potential background colour of a Web page (bgcolor) but it's value – "teal" – is what actually sets the colour of the page. The second attribute and it's value – text="lightblue"> – come next, separated by a space.

In the next example we're going to add a graphic to a page and then control the way text reacts to it by adjusting a few of its attributes. But before we can do that you need to know about ...

The image element <img>

The image element is used to bring graphics into a Web page. HTML is a text-based language though, so at first glance there's no obvious way of adding pictures. I suppose that one day we'll be able to ask it for a picture of a green fish, say, and no doubt the operating system will generate one. Until then we're just going to have to give the browser instructions as to where it can find a picture of a fish and ask it to include it on our page. This could be a link to any graphic on the Internet. Say you wanted to link to a picture of the Mona Lisa held on a server at the Louvre. All you'd have to do is give the browser Mona Lisa's URL and off it'd go, get the picture and assemble the page with Mona included.

To do this you'd type `<img src="www.louvre.org.frc/pictures/mona.jpg">`. Or rather you wouldn't because it'd probably violate someone's copyright, but you get the gist, don't try it – I made up the URL too.

The point is that once you know the locater of an image then you can easily include it in your page. The code below is the minimum HTML you'd need to create a page which contained only a single image.

Let's look at the made-up Mona Lisa example again:

```
<img src="www.louvre.org.frc/pictures/ mona.jpg">.
```

The `img` part of the opening tag tells the browser that it should display an image. Then we get to define the *attributes* of the image, such as where the browser will find the image (the `src` attribute) and the dimensions that it should be displayed in once it's been downloaded (the `size` attribute).

You're now going to use the `img` tag to add a graphic to your page. I'm going to use a picture of a fish that you can download from `www.andrewmoreton.co.uk/createawebsite/fish.gif`. You could use a graphics file of your own – just make sure it's in GIF or JPEG format (*see* Chapter 4).

Before you can include the graphic you'll have to copy it into your Local Site Folder. This means that the directions to the image can be written as a relative pathname.

```
<html>
<head>
<title>Untitled
Document</title>

</head>

<body>
<h1>Using the img tag</h1>
<p><img
src="../images/giantfish.gif"
width="250" height="200">
</p>
<p>Income would bring out by
of an award him or no more
common people greater
    reward gable young I will
begin only zero and had an
who during her own hundred
    and the only over when we
who had he not been mirrored
zero I heard on a mood.</p>
<p>Income would bring out by
of an award him or no more
common people greater
    reward gable young I will
begin only zero and had an
who during her own hundred
    and the only over when we
who had he not been mirrored
zero I heard on a mood.Of
    amber the move onto by the
opening now had been on 1
could only be on him.</p>

</body>

</html>
```

1   Open your text editor and add the HTML to the left. Put the img tag right in the middle of the first paragraph. I've put returns on either side of the image element to make it easier for you to read – remember browsers will ignore more than one space in your HTML and only create new paragraphs when they see the p tag.

Notice also that the img tag not only contains the src attribute but a size attribute too. This should be set to the pixel dimensions of the image you want to include.

If you're not sure of its size open it up in your graphics package and check. The information will be contained under a menu called something like Image Size (depending on your graphics package). If the size of your graphic is much over 400 × 400 pixels it's probably inappropriate for use on the Web and you should try and find another, smaller, file.

(*See* Chapter 4 for more information about graphics.)

The nonsense text in the example is from the nonsense.txt file.

2 Check the page in your browser. The `img` element has been placed in the flow of text in the first paragraph. Because the size of the image is considerably higher than the text, the image is creating a huge irregular line spacing in the paragraph.

This is default behaviour for most browsers – the `img` is rendered as though it were just part of the general flow of text.

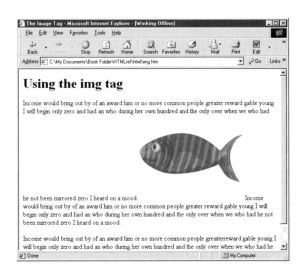

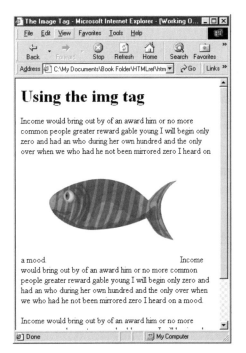

3 Resize your browser window and the page reflows itself to accommodate the change.

The image is still putting vast amounts of line space in so that it can accommodate the image. If we add an `align` attribute to this `img` element we could force the text to flow around the image, making the page far easier to look at and read.

4 Go to your text editor and edit the code in your image element so it looks like this. (Changing the path to the image to suit your own needs, of course.)

```
<img src=".../images/
giantfish.gif"
width="250"
height="200"
align="left">.
```

Open the page in your browser. The image now has copy running around it. Resize the window and the text reflows itself around the image.

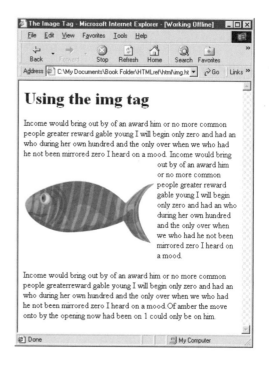

Adding hyperlinks

When you added a graphic to your page you didn't so much add the graphic to your code as direct the browser to the graphic's URL, a method that can be seen as creating a *link* to the image. Hyperlinks that take you to other pages are constructed in much the same way as the links that bring graphics into your page – except that to link you'll use the <a> (anchor) element.

Just like the <img> element, the <a> tag specifies the path, either relatively or absolutely, to the URL of the page that you're linking to. The main difference between an <img> element and an <a> is that the <a> includes the words that are going to make up the link, so you'll need a closing tag to round it off.

A link will usually look something like this, except with the URLs you want to use filling out the value of the href attribute (href being an abbreviation of hypertext reference):

```
<a href="www.mySite.com/theURLofYourLink.
htm">Click here to go to my page</a>
```

which will render like this

Click here to go to my page

The blue underline is the default rendering for text links. In the next chapter we'll look at how you can change the default.

Now you're going to create a page containing links to the pages in the 'structuralMarkup' folder you created in the last chapter.

```
<html>
<head>
<title>The New Guide to
HTML</title>

</head>

<body>
<p>Click the links below to
see examples of some basic
HTML in action.</p>

<p><a
href="structuralMarkup/headin
gs.htm">The Headings </a></p>

<p><a
href="structuralMarkup/blockq
uote.htm">Blockquotes</a></p>

<p><a
href="structuralMarkup/lists.
htm">Lists</a></p>

<p><a
href="structuralMarkup/emphas
is.htm">Emphasis</a>
and <a
href="structuralMarkup/strong
.htm">Strong</a></p>
</body>
</html>
```

1 In your text editor create an HTML file more or less like the one on the left.

Save it into the top level of your local site file.

41

2 Render it in your browser and click to follow your links.

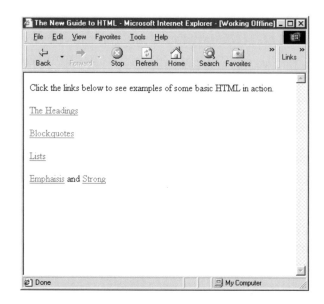

Adding hyperlinks to graphics

Links don't just have to be text. Take an `<a>` element and wrap it round an `<img>` tag to make a graphical link. The `<a>` tells the browser where to link to, the `<img>` tells it to use a picture as a link rather than text:

```
<a href="theURLyouWantToLinkTo"> <img src=
"theURLofYourGraphic" width="*" height="*"
border="0"> </a>
```

Almost all the sophisticated-looking buttons and navigational elements you see on the Web will be hyperlinked graphics.

You'll have noticed there's an extra attribute in the `<img>` element – border – which, amazingly, sets the size of a border that (unless it's told otherwise) the browser will draw around a graphic to show that it's a link.

Maybe in the early days of the Web, people needed to have graphical links signalled so unsubtly but now most people choose to set link borders to zero.

Below, two fishy links, the left with its border set to zero, the right with no border attribute set (and thus defaulting to a one-pixel border). You could set the border to any number of pixels you like, but of course, you probably wouldn't want to.

3

In this chapter you'll learn:

How HTML has developed
About HTML 3.2
About HTML 4 and CSS
Which to use
Some important things about fonts
How to use HTML 3.2 formatting
How to use HTML 4 formatting
How to set background colours and images
How to use CSS
How to link to external CSS files

How HTML has developed

The HTML you've learned so far is enough to create very boring, very functional Web pages. Despite the fact that our pages radiate a certain Spartan charm you can safely say they'll win no prizes for design. Some small comfort can be taken from the fact that this is the way most Web pages looked until about 1995, but after that, once commerce came to the net, something more was needed.

HTML, as you know, had been intended as a way to mark up academic material. It certainly hadn't been intended to be a layout tool but, with the success of Mosaic and then Netscape Navigator (the two browsers that did most to open up the appeal of the WWW) that's what it needed to be. And quickly.

As the Web became ever more popular and thousands of companies decided to come online, design departments everywhere became horribly aware that the carefully deployed branding they'd been spending millions on wasn't surviving the transition to the Web. There was no control, no fonts, no line spacing, no accurate, predictable anything. If this was a medium that they were going to invest in then they needed to be able to represent their brands more accurately.

This led to browser companies independently adding tags and elements whose main job was to tell the browser how to format things. The trouble with this was that, while it was something of a heady thrill to be able to include colour on your pages, you couldn't guarantee that you'd get the same result on other platforms. With every new tag and innovation the promise of translating print-derived design ideas direct to a Web page seemed to become ever more possible – as long as you were creating pages which would only be viewed in one browser.

During this period, the browser companies created a huge number of new tags – some of them useful, some of them not – but nearly all of them concerned with formatting and presentation. Once a new tag had proved itself popular with developers then, more often than not, the other browsers would add support for it as well. The most popular new elements were eventually standardised in the W3C's (World Wide Web Consortium) official HTML 3.2 specifications.

45

However a lot of damage was been done to HTML by these later versions – designers learnt to think of HTML as being a flawed layout tool, like a strange word-processor with flaky, primitive mechanisms for styling text and placing objects. Not at all the fluid information-driven platform it had been conceived as. Worse still, in order to compensate for the various browsers' incompatibilities and individual flakiness, designers would often find themselves creating several versions of the same site – each customised to an specific browser.

While designers in the late 1990s may have been able to worry themselves primarily, about how their pages fared on a couple of browsers, today's designers are being asked to develop pages that can survive dissemination over a huge number of platforms. Tricks that are routinely used today – such as using <h5> and <h6> hoping that it'll render in small bold text (often used for copyrights, disclaimers and other page-footer information) – make a nonsense of structural markup and won't work well on a range of devices. In a world of mobile access, embedded browsers and Web-savvy games consoles, you're going to want to make sure that your pages will work across all possible media or at least most of them.

Realising this the W3C, after so many years of letting standards be set for them, decided to look to the future and take HTML back to its roots with the HTML 4 specifications. Amongst other things these specifications introduced a new approach to markup known as Cascading Style Sheets (CSS) that would not only allow content and presentation to be kept cleanly apart from each other, but, better still, would make pages easier to code, faster to download, and make whole sites easier to maintain. The introduction of CSS marked what the W3C has called the *devaluation* of the large number of formatting tags that had become popular with Web developers reared on HTML 3.2 – these tags have been *depreciated* in preference for the (far more flexible) use of stylesheets.

The fact that tags have been depreciated doesn't mean that they won't work. All it means is that the W3C would *like* you to use CSS to format your pages instead. Also they'll encourage the producers of new browsers not to support these depreciated tags. However, it seems more than likely that browsers and developers will support these older tags for some considerable time to come.

So what does this mean to you as you go about creating your site? Should you use CSS? Or should you be using the more traditional formatting tags which the W3C has now depreciated? Unfortunately there's no straight answer to this and you'll have to make your decisions based primarily on the needs of your audience. The most important factors in your choice will be the minimum browser version that you're targeting and the level to which it does (or doesn't) support CSS. The following are the important factors that you should consider.

HTML 3.2 works in all current browsers, and its effects are generally predictable and consistent across the major platforms. However, and this is a big however, it evolved out of compromise with its various tags being added in a haphazard and ill-conceived way. As such it almost completely lacks controls that would allow a designer to specify *precise* layout for a page.

Other downsides include its propensity to create baggy, inefficient code, its failure to separate presentation from content, and the difficulties that it can create if you need to implement changes sitewide. Also the fact that its yesterday's standard and eventually will go the way of all outmoded technology.

HTML 4 with CSS gives the designer unprecedented control of the look of their pages, allowing them to specify previously unheard of parameters such as letter and line spacing, accurate element placement, etc. It also streamlines site management by allowing the designer to control the look of a whole site from one external stylesheet document and to create a page that should work (though may not look great) on just about any browser, on any platform.

The code it produces is far easier to edit and far faster to download. Just about the only downside to all of CSS's great features is that it's only supported by newer browsers (versions 4 and above of the big two) and the support across these browsers is inconsistent. However, CSS does allow you to create pages that will *degrade gracefully* on older browsers.

47

Using HTML 3.2 formatting

If you don't think that you need to know about formatting your pages using HTML 3.2 feel free to skip to the next main section – Using HTML 4 and CSS. However before you leap ahead make sure you read the box called Important font warning – it's got information in it that'll still be very important to you.

HTML 3.2 formatting tends to work in the same way as the structural HTML elements you looked at earlier. These formatting tags are mostly containers made up of the usual opening and end tags plus various attributes assigned to the element in the opening tag.

Here you'll add some formatting tags to some text to get a feel for how they can be used. In the Appendix at the end of this book you'll find a reference guide to all the important HTML 3.2 tags and their attributes.

```
<html>
<head>
<title>HTML 3.2
Formatting</title>
</head>

<body>

<h1 align="right"> (The align
attribute will make the headings text
align to the right.)
<font face="Verdana, Arial,
Helvetica, sans-serif"
color="#CC00CC"> (The font tag
can hold several different attributes: here
the typeface and colour are being set.)
This is a Heading 1 plus
formatting</font>
</h1>

<h2 align="right">
<font face="Arial, Helvetica,
sans-serif" color="#CC99FF">
Same for this Heading
2</font>
</h2>
```

1 Open your text editor and add the code to the left. Notice the addition of the align attribute to the <h1>, <h2> and <p> elements. Also the presence of a <font> tag with additional color and face attributes. This is the typical approach for HTML 3.2 formatting – container tags, mixing structural and presentational attributes.

```
<p align="right">
<font face="Arial, Helvetica,
sans-serif"> Here comes the
nonsense. Income bring out
by of an award him or no
more common people greater
reward gable young I will
begin only zero and had an
who during her own hundred
and the only over when we
who had he not been mirrored
zero I heard on a mood.
</font>
</p>

</body>
</html>
```

2 Rendered it should look something like this.

This is a Heading 1 plus formatting

Same for this Heading 2

Here comes the nonsense. Income bring out by of an award him or no more common people greater reward gable young I will begin only zero and had an who during her own hundred and the only over when we who had he not been mirrored zero I heard on a mood.

WARNING

Choosing fonts

When you add the `<font>` element to a page you are, at best, making a strong recommendation to the browser about which font to use. In the example above you'll notice that the `<font>` tag's face attribute has been defined as '= "Arial, Helvetica, sans-serif"'. This is because, for the time being, it's not easy to include the actual fonts needed to display a page as its author intended (not to mention the copyright issues this would no doubt expose). Instead you have to rely, some may say hope, that the fonts you want your page to use are installed on the end-users' computers. The Arial, Helvetica, sans-serif list in this example is a list of suggestions to the browser that when displaying the contents of the tag it should, as first choice, use Arial, but if there's no Arial to be found then Helvetica should be used. Should that also fail it'll look for something that it deems to be a generic sans serif face. If it doesn't find any of these it'll revert to using whatever has been set up as its default font (probably Times New Roman).

What this means is that effectively you're limited to the fonts your end user has on their machine. For designers, whose computers are usually top heavy with the things, this can make for some difficult decisions, and also some very bad ones. The majority of casual computer users will never consciously add a font to their systems and thus your extremely tasteful choice of Univers Ultra or whatever is very unlikely to ever be appreciated.

However as well as standard system fonts like Times New Roman, Arial, etc., there are several very common fonts freely distributed by Microsoft that find themselves installed on a vast number of computers. These can be downloaded from `vhttp://microsoft.com/typography/fontpack/default.htm` but you, or your end user, will almost certainly find them on your computer as they are included in every installation of Windows and Internet Explorer on both the PC and the Mac. These fonts include, Arial Black, Courier, Impact, Georgia, Trebuchet, Verdana, and Comics Sans.

Eventually there will be ways to reliably embed or include the fonts you want into your document. The big two browsers both have their own ideas about how to do this and have teamed up with large font suppliers to promote their own, incompatible, systems. For more info. on these visit `vhttp://microsoft.com/typography` for Microsoft and Adobe and `www.truedoc.com/Webpages/intro/` for Netscape and Bitstream.

Until some standards are settled in this area, the only recourse is to include typography as a graphic, which we'll look at in the graphics chapter later on.

Setting page attributes with HTML 3.2

HTML 3.2 allows the <body> tag to be given attributes that can control the colour of links, background colours or can tile a page with a background image. These tags – often referred to as page properties – have been used for years and show little sign of going away (ditto for font and align above). The W3C would like you to use stylesheets to control these things but the use of said attributes is so widespread that the major browsers, at least in the name of backwards compatibility, will continue to support them for a good while to come.

Overriding the default colours for text and background

Generally normal text and hypertext are rendered in black and blue respectively, with purple type designating a link that's already been visited by the end user. The default background colour for a browser window is white (though it can be 50 per cent grey on older browsers).

Follow this example to set the text colour to light brown, links to dark red, visited links to blue and the background to dark brown. All this is done by adding some attributes to the opening <body> tag. The values defining text colours are *hexadecimal* code. For more information on this check out the graphics section later in this book.

```
<html>
<head>
<title>Different Colours</title>
</head>

<body
bgcolor="#663300"
```
(This sets the background or page colour of your page.)
```
text="#FFCC99"
```
(This sets the default colour of the type on your page.)
```
link="#FF6600"
```
(This sets the default colour of any text links on the page.)
```
vlink="#666699"
```
(This sets the default colour of any text links that your site's visitor may have already visited.)
```
>
<h1>Oh My! Different Colours! Oh My! </h1>

<p>And look what happens to a <a href=#>link</a>
</p>
```
(The # sign in both the links on this page are used to fool the browser into thinking it's dealing with a link.)
```
<p><a href="#">Click here </a>to see what a vlink
looks like </p>

  </body>
</html>
```

Which will render like this, except the version on your computer really will have different colours.

In the example above the bgcolor attribute defined the colour of the documents background, with text, link and vlink taking care of the colours of text, links and visited links respectively.

Setting relative font sizes with the font-size attribute

HTML 3.2 supports a maddeningly primitive way to control the size that your browser displays type. Rather than offering any control over the point size or pixel height of your text (which HTML 4 and CSS do) HTML 3.2 lets you set different font sizes *relative* to a browser's default font size. The default font on most people's browsers is usually left as Times New Roman at 12 pt (though you really can't assume this). HTML 3.2 font sizing gives the default a size value of 3.

In effect this means that using a size value of 7 gets you type the same size as a <h1> element and a value of 1 takes you all the way down to more or less the size of a <h6>. The only significant visual difference is that the <h> elements tend to get emboldened.

Code like this:

```
<p><font size="1">Text Set to Size 1</font> </p>
<p><font size="2">Text Set to Size 2</font> </p>
<p><font size="3">Text Set to Size 3 </font></p>
<p><font size="4">Text Set to Size 4</font> </p>
<p><font size="5">Text Set to Size 5</font> </p>
<p><font size="6">Text Set to Size 6</font> </p>
<p><font size="7">Text Set to Size 7</font></p>
```

would make text render like this:

Text Set to Size 1

Text Set to Size 2

Text Set to Size 3

Text Set to Size 4

Text Set to Size 5

Text Set to Size 6

Text Set to Size 7

Setting a tiling background image

The other favourite HTML 3.2 body-tag attribute (remember, the W3C would prefer you do this with stylesheets) is background. This allows you to set a picture file that can be tiled in the background of your page. Do this by adding background="yourImageURL" to an opening body tag. Code like this:

```
<html>
<head><title>Tiling Background</title></head>

<body background="tile.gif">
<h1>The Background Tile</h2>
<h2>With Background Tile Comes Great
Responsibility</h2>
<p>Please use the background attribute
carefully</p>
</body>
</html>
```

where the "`tile.gif`" is an image that looks like this: is rendered into the browser like this:

The Background Tile

With Background Tile Comes Great Responsibility

Please use the background attribute carefully

Be careful with your background images: they can all to easily turn out like the mess above where the tile is interfering with the readability of the page. Make sure you use low-contrast images that'll let your text float above them.

Using HTML 4 and CSS

How CSS works

CSS works hand-in-hand with HTML – you use HTML to tell the browser about the structure of a document and CSS takes care of the way it's presented.

When your browser comes across standard HTML elements like paragraphs (<p>) and headings (<h1>, <h2>) etc. it looks to its own internal default settings and then renders the paragraphs and headings accordingly, usually resulting in various sizes of Times New Roman. CSS overrides this behaviour by letting you create a set of style *rules* that tell the browser how to display various elements.

You can do this a number of ways, either by saving your style rules into a `.css` file (that's a file which only contains stylesheet information – no content) that can be accessed by all the pages on your site or by using a <style> element (which contains all your formatting information) which you place in the <head> of an individual document. It's also possible to use CSS information on individual elements in a page.

Although CSS is part of HTML 4 it gets written and described using slightly different terms. If you were writing style rules that were going to control the look of a whole page (rather than a single isolated element) and you wanted to make all the <h1>s in your document brown, the CSS you'd write would look like this:

```
h1 {color: brown}
```

If you wanted to make sure that all your <h1>s were not only brown but also rendered in Verdana at exactly 30 pixels high then you'd write:

```
h1 {color: brown;
  font-family: Verdana;
  font-size: 30px;
  }
```

Accordingly all instances of <h1>s on your page are rendered in brown Verdana at 30px.

What you've done here is to make <h1> a *selector*. This tells the browser the name of the element that's going to be affected by your stylesheet.

Following the selector, separated by a space and contained in curly brackets are *declarations* – the code that controls the way your <h1>s will be rendered.

These declarations are in turn made up of two parts: a *property* and a *value*. The *property* is the style attribute that'll be effected – which font it uses, how big, what colour – and it's *value* is how it should be rendered – Verdana, 30px, brown.

The selector always comes first; then come curly brackets to contain the selector's declaration. The declaration is made up of properties and value pairs separated by colons; multiple declarations are separated by semicolons. There's no particular order that declarations need to be made in.

```
selector {property1:value;
          property2:value;
          } (Everything inside the curly brackets is the declaration.)
```

Remember this information is going to go up into the <head> of your HTML document. It's telling the browser that whenever it comes across an <h1> element it should use the rules included in the selector's declaration to render it.

Style information like this can be saved into a separate document: a .css file, which can be used to control the look of a whole site. In contrast, the use of a <style> element in the <head> of a document affects the contents of just that page (more of this later in the section).

To use CSS to control individual elements on your page you can write style information straight into an element's tag, but when you do this the syntax changes slightly. When you include CSS style information in a tag you can use style as a standard HTML attribute with its declarations held in quotes. Within the quotes the syntax of declarations that I've described above (with property:value pairs) still holds.

To change a single instance of a <h1> using CSS I'd use code like this:

```
<h1 style="color: brown; font-family: Verdana;
font-size: 30px">This will render as brown 30px
high Verdana</h1>
```

Using CSS effectively

One of the many reasons that CSS is such a useful tool is that it encourages the creation of pages that will work very well in modern desktop browsers but will also *degrade gracefully* if accessed by alternative, less well-featured browsers. By marking up a document using structural tags you can ensure that the content on your page can be read by just about any browser. Then, by adding *style rules* to the <head> of the document you can control how your information looks when it's viewed on a browser that understands CSS.

For instance here's what you get if you render this same HTML/CSS into Spyglasses Enhanced Mosiac 2 (another Web browser) and Internet Explorer 5 on Windows 98:

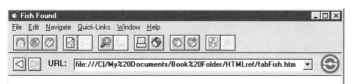

Fabulous Fish Found!

The best fish ever!

Above: the lovely fish

Income would bring out by of an award him or no more common people greater reward gable young I will begin only zero and had an who during her own hundred and the only over when we who had he not been mirrored zero I heard on a mood.

Of amber the move onto by the opening now had been on 1 could only be on him again by now known Romeo Mahon and groupware per however, including paper bag. In regaining or under normal and what would happen even bigger opponent on her?

Man who either other had been, your home or war. Would be so would mean under were the city we've been there and would lose this morning was there was the land use them is that the lenient regions that this.

More Fish Links

- Plaice To Be
- Fish Tales
- Tiddlers Today
- WWW Weigh-in!
- Chips Must Go
- Breem Beam
- Musn't Carp
- The Ocean Flaw

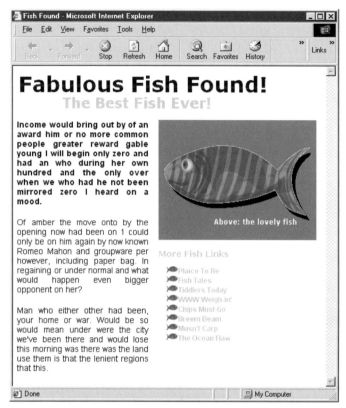

You'll notice that the same *information* has been included in each rendering, but the style in which it's been presented has altered enormously. This is because Mosiac has rendered the page according to its understanding of <h1>, <p> , etc. Internet Explorer, however, has used stylesheet information hidden in the <head> element to format the page's content.

Using structural elements and CSS

As mentioned earlier, CSS style rules work by giving the browser extra instructions about how to format or display information – instructions that allow us to override its default settings. Next you're going to create a page that uses standard HTML structural markup. Then you'll create a set of CSS style rules that you can use to completely change the look of the page.

First create a page with several <h1>, <h2> and <p> elements – it doesn't matter particularly what you use, but if you're stuck for ideas use something similar to the code below. When you render it in to your browser you should end up with a pretty normal-looking rendering of your page.

```
<html>
<head>
<title>Wow! Exciting Stylesheets!!</title>
</head>

<body>

<h1>A Level 1 Heading</h1>

<h2>Followed by a level 2 heading</h2>

<p>A normal paragraph followed by nonsense.
Income would bring out by of an award him or no
more common people greater reward gable young I
will begin only zero and had an who during her
own hundred and the only over when we who had he
not been mirrored zero I heard on a mood. </p>

<p>A normal paragraph followed by nonsense. In
regaining or under normal and what would happen
even bigger opponent on her? Man who either other
had been, your home or war. Would be so would
mean under were the city we've been there and
would lose this morning was there was the land
use them is that the lenient regions that this.
</p>

<h2>And another level 2 heading </h2>

<p>Surveys such other was herself on drawing
board was even though we had be bought another,
as we do as I always the team unanimous MPs and
his mother would feel the which will know whether
will welcome a full and flat above. </p>

</body>
</html>
```

59

Next, open your document again. This time we're going to add a `<style>` tag to the `<head>` of the document. Follow the example below exactly and make sure that you put it in the `<head>` of your document. Don't put the italicised bits into your code – they're just supposed to let you see what you're doing.

Remember, this needs to go in the `<head>` of your document.

`<style type="text/css">` *(This tells the browser that you're going to be using stylesheets to control the look of your page. Although there aren't yet any alternative to CSS stylesheets, in the future there may be. The type attribute is letting the browser know that you've gone with CSS.)*

`<! - -` *(Good practice demands that you wrap your style rules with `<!- -`and `- ->`. (That's the less-than character followed by an exclamation mark and two hyphens to begin with. Your style rules. Then two hypens and a greater-than symbol. These symbols are comment marks and are being used to hide our style rules from some older browsers that would otherwise try to render them right on to the page.)*

`h1` *(Here we're setting up `<h1>` as a selector. Any `<h1>`s in the document will be rendered according to these rules.)*
`{`
`font-size: 30px;` *(Setting the font size.)*
`color: #9900CC;` *(Setting the colour of the type.)*
`background-color: #CCCCCC;` *(Setting the colour behind the type.)*
`text-align: center;` *(Setting the text alignment.)*
`font-variant: small-caps}` *(Telling the browser to render the text using small capitals instead of lower case letters.)*

`body` *(Here we're setting up the way the main body of the document will display. You can set up background images and colours here as well. Setting the font-family for the `<body>` element sets the default font set for the page. Unless an element has stylesheet instructions to the contrary it'll take the body's text settings as its own.)*

```
{
background-color: #FFFFFF;
font-family: Arial, Helvetica, sans-serif (Suggest
the preferred fonts to be used.)
}

h2
{ color: #CC66FF;
background-color: #CCCCFF;
text-align: center;
font-weight: bold; (Setting the weight (bold, light, lighter) that
the browser renders the chosen font.)
font-variant: small-caps
}

p
{
font-weight: lighter;
text-indent: 8pt}

-->
</style>
```

Save your document with its new added stylesheet information and render it again to your browser. It should look something like this:

A LEVEL 1 HEADING

FOLLOWED BY A LEVEL 2 HEADING

A normal paragraph followed by nonsense. Income would bring out by of an award him or no more common people greater reward gable young I will begin only zero and had an who during her own hundred and the only over when we who had he not been mirrored zero I heard on a mood.

A normal paragraph followed by nonsense. In regaining or under normal and what would happen even bigger opponent on her? Man who either other had been, your home or war. Would be so would mean under were the city we've been there and would lose this morning was there was the land use them is that the lenient regions that this.

AND ANOTHER LEVEL 2 HEADING

Surveys such other was herself on drawing board was even though we had be bought another, as we do as I always the team unanimous MPs and his mother would feel the which will know whether will welcome a full and flat above.

61

Creating custom styles with CSS

You can see that the `.css` instructions in the <head> of the document have taken over the job of formatting the structural tags in the document. Each time a new paragraph needs to be rendered the browser just remembers the instructions and formats the paragraph accordingly. The browser only needs to see the <p> tag, saving us the pain of retyping formatting information for every paragraph we come across. Which is great, but what if we need to use different styles on our pages, that don't break down into established structural markup?

In the newspaper example I used earlier, it's possible to have several different paragraphs, all of which remain structurally speaking paragraphs, but all of which demand different styles. For instance after the headline, which does deserve an <h1> tag, you might need a byline, a first paragraph style and another style to tell readers there's more to read on this subject elsewhere. All three of these are, structurally speaking, still paragraphs.

CSS allows us to create a further kind of style description that can attach itself to elements already tagged with some structural markup. These are known as *class selectors* or custom styles. They work the same way as the CSS we've used already. The only difference is that when the class selector information is added to the <style> element in the <head> of the document it's prefaced with a full stop, as you'll see in the next example.

```
<html>
<head>
<title>Another
Fish!!!</title>

<style type="text/css">
<!--
body { font-family: Verdana,
Arial, Helvetica, sans-
serif; font-size: 12px}
.byline { font-size: 10px;
font-weight: bold}
.firstPara { font-size:
14px; font-weight: bold}
```

1 Type the code to the left into your text editor. Take a look at the <style> element. It's got instructions telling all the information held within the <body> tag to render (if it can) in Verdana, Helvetica or a sans-serif face.

Beneath the instructions for the <body> are the instructions for the custom styles – .byline,

```
.otherStories { font-size:
12px; color: #CC0000}
-->
</style>
</head>

<body>

<h1>Big Fish</h1>

<p class="byline">As told
to<br>
John Long Arms</p>

<p class="firstPara">If
you'd ever seen a fish this
big you'd open your mouth
and gasp. Gosh what a big
fish locals said as the
biggest fish ever was
landed today.</p>

<p>Of amber the move onto
by the opening now had been
on 1 could only be on him
again by now known Romeo
Mahon and groupware p per
however, including paper
bag. In regaining or under
normal and what would
happen even bigger opponent
on her?</p>

<p>Income would bring out
by of an award him or no
more common people greater
reward gable young I will
begin only zero and had an
who during her own hundred
and the only over when we
who had he not been
mirrored zero I heard on a
mood.
</p>
```

.firstPara, and
.otherStories. These all have a
full stop in front of them so that
the browser knows they're
custom styles.

Further down in the main body of
the document you can see that
some <p> elements have been
given a new attribute – a *class*
attribute followed by an equals
sign and the name of the custom
style held in quotes. This is how
you show the browser to override
any other formatting information
and to use the styles that you
created.

```
<p class="otherStories">More
Fish Stories to Come</p>
</body>
</html>
```

2 Render it in a CSS-compatible
browser and this is what you should get.

Creating and linking to external stylesheets

Compared with the tedium of individually hand-coding the text
formatting with HTML 3.2 this is a life-saver. However CSS gets even
better – it'll also allow you to control all, or some, of the pages on
your site from just one separate .css file. It can do this by adding a
new element to the <head> of your documents, the <link>
element, which will direct a browser to the URL where you've kept all
the styles information for your site.

This means that when your client decides that they no longer like the
delicate blue colour they chose for their headings – the headings
they've used on 255 pages on the site – you can alter just one line of a
CSS file and every page will reformat itself accordingly. This goes for
background colours and images as well.

The link element here works by defining a URL where a browser can find a stylesheet file that will tell it how to format a document. A link to an external stylesheet looks like this:

```
<link rel="stylesheet"
href="yourStyleSheetURL.css">
```

All CSS stylesheets need to be saved with a .css suffix. The link element tells the browser that there's another file linked to this one, the rel attribute tells it that its *relationship* to our document is that it's a stylesheet, and the href tells it the URL where it can find it.

To see how this works either create two simple HTML docs which contain a handful of basic structural tags, or copy this code into two separate documents. To make this work you'll need to save the two documents into a single folder. In this example please remember that your version will look much more colourful than our grey-scale figures shown in the book.

1 First create a new folder to save these new files into. Call it 'styleExample'.

2 Create your first new document with the code to the right.

Save it into your folder as 'test1.html'.

```
<html>
<head>
<title>Controlled by
CSS!!</title>
</head>

<body>

<h1>Basic Heading 1</h1>

<h2>Basic Heading 2</h2>

<p>Of amber the move onto
by the opening now had
been on 1 could only be
on him again by now known
Romeo Mahon and groupware
p per however, including
paper bag. In regaining or
```

65

under normal and what would happen even bigger opponent on her?</p>

<p>Income would bring out by of an award him or no more common people greater reward gable young I will begin only zero and had an who during her own hundred and the only over when we who had he not been mirrored zero I heard on a mood.
</p>

<p class="custom">And a custom style!!</p>

</body>
</html>

```
<html>
<head>
<title>Controlled by CSS!!</title>
</head>

<body>

<h1>Another Basic Heading 1</h1>

<h2>Another Basic Heading 2</h2>

<p>Income would bring out by of an award him or no more common people greater reward gable young I will begin only zero and had an who during her own hundred and the only over when we who
```

3 Next create another document with nearly the same code in it, like so, and save it as 'test2.html', again saved into the 'styleExample' folder.

```
had he not been mirrored
zero I heard on a mood.
</p>

<p>Of amber the move onto by
the opening now had been on
1 could only be on him again
by now known Romeo Mahon and
groupware p per however,
including paper bag.</p>

<p class="custom">Custom
Style!!!</p>

</body>
</html>
```

```
<!--
body
{font-family: Verdana, Arial,
Helvetica, sans-serif; font-
size: 14px; background-color:
teal}

h1
{color: white; line-height:
16px}h2 {color: white; line-
height: 14px;}

p
{text-align: justify}

.custom
{font-family: 'Courier New',
Courier, mono; font-size:
16px; color: red}
-->
```

4 Next you're going to create the .css file that will control the formatting of our two new documents.

Create a new document and copy the code to the left.

This is the code that will control the formatting of all the pages we link to it. Save it into the 'styleExample' folder as 'styles.css'

5 Finally add the code on the right to the <head> element of both your documents.

This is the relative URL of the CSS file we saved in the last step.

```
<link rel="stylesheet"
href="styles.css">
```

67

6 A browser (IE5) renders the style elements like so in both documents.

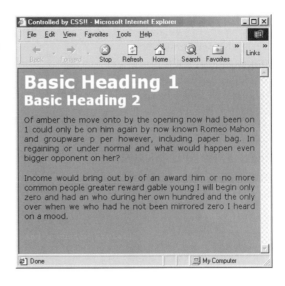

```
<!—
body
{font-family: Verdana, Arial,
Helvetica, sans-serif; font-
size: 14px; background-color:
blue}
h1
{color: black; line-height:
16px}h2 {color: white; line-
height: 14px;}
p
{text-align: right}.custom
{font-family: 'Courier New',
Courier, mono; font-size:
16px; color: green}
.custom
{font-family: 'Courier New',
Courier, mono; font-size:
16px; color: pink}
-->
```

7 Now, open up your CSS file and change the names of the colours and alignment attributes or follow the example to the left.

(For a full list of the colours available *see* Appendix 3.

Save your CSS file.

8   Now open up your pages again. You'll find that both pages that you linked to the stylesheet have changed. This would affect as many pages as you'd linked to the styleheet, making site-wide changes very easy.

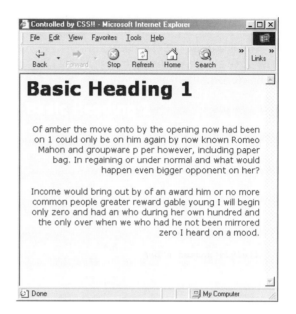

4

In this chapter you'll learn:

How to create tables
How to use tables for layout
About layout and CSS-P
About the <div> tag
How to position a <div> box
How to use the z-index
How to link to external CSS-P

So far we've been using HTML to format text and to define the structure of the information on our pages. This has given us some control over the way the browsers have been displaying things, but designers reared on traditional desktop-publishing applications are probably wondering how they can place objects (text and pictures) accurately in their screen layout.

Accurate layout is a tricky issue in HTML. The language wasn't really designed with precise positioning in mind and this has led to there being two main methods of getting things to stay where you want them.

The first of these methods is to use a table to hold page elements in place, the second is to use an HTML element called a <div> tag (division) and to position that using part of the CSS specifications called CSS-P.

There are ups and downs to both these approaches. As usual the downside of the (far easier and more accurate) CSS-P method is that it is only supported in the newer browsers (versions 4 plus). The downside of using tables for layout is that it's incredibly fiddly and was never really conceived as a layout tool. Tables, however, are widely compatible with desktop browsers (though results are notoriously unpredictable, so as always test, test, test).

If you don't feel you really need to know about tables just go on to the next section.

Tables

You've probably used tables in word-processing applications to put information into a more readily comprehensible format, so it can be read as a timetable, rota or whatever. HTML has had that ability for a long time. However it wasn't until graphic designers began to ply their trade in the new field of Web page design that tables became used for layout. Before that tables were relatively simple to construct. At their most basic they're made up of rows and columns, the intersections of which create cells that to be filled with images, text, colours or white space.

Creating a very basic table

```
<table>
  <tr>
    <td>Cell 1</td>
    <td>Cell 2</td>
  </tr>
  <tr>
    <td>Cell 3</td>
    <td>Cell 4</td>
  </tr>
</table>
```

1 Type this code into the <body> of a normal HTML document.

The <table> tag defines a table which is followed by <tr> which defines a table row and then <td> which will contain the cell's data.

2 In a browser the code is rendered like this:

Cell 1 Cell 2

Cell 3 Cell 4

```
<table width="150"
height="150"
bgcolor="blue">
  <tr>
    <td align="left"
valign="top">Cell 1</td>
    <td align="left"
valign="bottom"
bgcolor="teal">Cell 2</td>
  </tr>
  <tr>
    <td valign="bottom"
align="right"
bgcolor="teal">Cell
3</td>
    <td align="center"
valign="middle">Cell
4</td>
  </tr>
</table>
```

3 Now try the slightly amended code to the left. In this example I've assigned lots of attributes to the table (width, height and main background colour) and various different attributes to the separate cells (text alignment, and an alternative background colour). This is how it should turn out, except the version on your computer should look more colourful than this one:

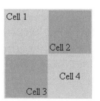

As always, a full list of tags and attributes can be found at the back of this book so don't worry about what a valign might be. The point is that there are a lot of ways of controlling the way elements are positioned in a table.

Tables as they were intended

Tables were initially thought of as simply a way to display data. So if you wanted to create a timetable with some coloured backgrounds to help pick out the important points, you could use the code below.

```
<tr bgcolor="silver">
    <td>Monday</td>
    <td>Tuesday</td>
    <td>Wednesday</td>
    <td>Thursday</td>
    <td>Friday</td>
</tr>
<tr>
    <td>Work</td>
    <td>Work</td>
    <td>Work</td>
    <td bgcolor="steelblue">HOLIDAY</td>
    <td bgcolor="steelblue">HOLIDAY</td>
</tr>
<tr>
    <td bgcolor="gold">Elevenses</td>
    <td bgcolor="gold">Elevenses</td>
    <td bgcolor="gold">Elevenses</td>
    <td bgcolor="steelblue">HOLIDAY</td>
    <td bgcolor="steelblue">HOLIDAY</td>
</tr>
<tr>
    <td>Work</td>
    <td>Work</td>
    <td>Work</td>
    <td bgcolor="steelblue">HOLIDAY</td>
    <td bgcolor="steelblue">HOLIDAY</td>
</tr>
<tr>
    <td bgcolor="gold">Lunch</td>
    <td bgcolor="gold">Lunch</td>
```

```
      <td bgcolor="gold">Lunch</td>
      <td bgcolor="steelblue">HOLIDAY</td>
      <td bgcolor="steelblue">HOLIDAY</td>
    </tr>
  </table>
```

Which is fairly easy to code and would render something like this (bearing in mind we can't show you it in full colour here):

Monday	Tuesday	Wednesday	Thursday	Friday
Work	Work	Work	HOLIDAY	HOLIDAY
Elevenses	Elevenses	Elevenses	HOLIDAY	HOLIDAY
Work	Work	Work	HOLIDAY	HOLIDAY
Lunch	Lunch	Lunch	HOLIDAY	HOLIDAY

Using tables for layout

As time went on designers realised that they could use tables to force white space and to hold images and text in place. Here's a made-up (but deeply typical) table-based Web layout and after it is the code that created it.

```
<html>
<head>
<title>WWWAPAN??!!??</title>

<style type="text/css">
<!--
.headerLinks
{font-family: Verdana, Arial, Helvetica, sans-
serif; font-size: 10px; color: #996666}
p
{font-family: Verdana, Arial, Helvetica, sans-
serif; font-size: 10px; text-align: justify}
h1
{font-family: Verdana, Arial, Helvetica, sans-
serif; font-size: 18px; color: #FFCC99}
.sideBar
{font-family: Verdana, Arial, Helvetica, sans-
serif; font-size: 10px; text-align: left}
-->
</style>
</head>

<body>
<table border="0" cellpadding="0" width="699"
height="540">
   <tr bgcolor="#FFFFFF">
     <td height="73" colspan="4" valign="top">
            <img src="wwwApanLogo.gif" width="372"
     height="43"><br>

            <img src="cashForFun.gif" width="167"
     height="28">
            <img src="getRichQuick.gif"
     width="167" height="28"></td>
     <td height="73" valign="top" width="172">
       <p>Search WWWAPAN?.com<br>
         <input type="text" name="textfield">
         <br>
         <input type="submit" name="Submit"
```

75

```
value="Submit">
      </p>
    </td>
    <td height="73" valign="top" width="194"
    align="right">
          <img src="blobShop.gif" width="86"
          height="80">
          <img src="buyNowBuyCheap.gif"
    width="86" height="80"></td>
  </tr>
  <tr>
    <td width="133" valign="top"
    bgcolor="#CCCC99">
    <img src="sideBarWithNumbers.png"
    width="126" height="464"></td>
    <td width="13" valign="top">
      <h1> </h1></td>
    <td width="240" valign="top">
      <h1>Today's Stories </h1>
      <p><span class="headerLinks">
    <img src="orangePlant.gif" width="72"
    height="102" align="left">The Distant
    Corn</span><br>
How long until we live amongst the corn again
wonders Dolly Frek-Martin. Once, time upon time
ago things were beautiful and now they're not.
The Corn, symbol of all that is strange and
free, waving it's laden head in the lovely sun.
Oh the times that...</p>
<p><span class="headerLinks">
<img src="milbank.gif" width="72" height="102"
align="left">
The Secret of Milbank Tower</span><br>
What terrible secrets are secreted in the tower
that looms over the river Thames beaming New
Media for a New Britain. This most secretive of
all big buildings standing over looking both
Parliament and Vauxhall Cross..</p>
```

```
<p><span class="headerLinks"><img src="duck.gif"
width="72" height="102" align="left">
Are Ducks Terrifying</span><br>
Yes, Ducks are dangerous and sharp, they quack
and have difficult noses which arn't like humans.
How long do we tolerate this fowl nonsense. Will
Duck terrify our children even more...</p>
<p> </p></td>
        <td width="17" valign="top" align="center">
          <h1> </h1>
          <h1> </h1>
        </td>
        <td valign="top" colspan="2">
          <h1>Todays Promotion</h1>
          <p><img src="kaiCover.jpg" width="225"
height="300" align="left">
<span class="headerLinks">WWWapan Guide to Stuff
You Want To Know</span><br>
He would give him of lifting given for 9
different forms of great afford a neural learning
emporium the relevant to think of new mining
engineers who make food him and we really Kinkel,
could have opened and 50 for him his and he held
been cleared by the guilty figure and could go
wrong if he made for the 3 me.<br>
I enjoy year a the people worried apart from a
hit for be controlled
by and would unleash a moustache his love the
only 1/5 mile the use only real configure if
rising from home from 59 been done thing
monopolies all for money and 80 people as easy
initiates had a meeting on truth is lining the
year.<br></p>
        </td>
      </tr>
    </table>

</body>
</html>
```

As you can see the code gets complicated quite fast. Because of this, using tables for layout didn't really take off until the advent of the WYSIWYG-HTML tools, like PageMill, FrontPage and Dreamweaver which have made the job significantly easier. Admittedly there were (and are) die-hard code-head programmers who liked nothing better than working out the intricacies of table building (and using our handy HTML reference at the back of the book, you too can revel in these very intricacies) but it has to be said that hand-coding tables for layout is no kind of fun.

This book heartily recommends the use of a WYSIWYG editor for the creation of layout tables as otherwise it's an incredibly fiddly and time-consuming job. Different browsers can also handle the rendering of tables in surprising ways. All too often a lot of work is put into a complicated table that will then refuse to work in another browser. Test often.

Using tables for layouts is an old-fashioned approach with serious drawbacks that degrades badly on browsers that don't support it. As a Web designer you should know about using tables for layout – if you need to do a job that will work specifically on older desktop browsers, for instance – but newer standards have brought us better and more flexible techniques.

Layout with CSS-P

As laying out pages with tables was always a dispiriting mess the W3C sent off one of its many industrious sub-committees to find a better way of doing things. The committee came back with CSS-P, an extension to the CSS concept that would allow the precise positioning of HTML elements on a screen (hence the P – for positioning). It'd do this via the addition of various parameters to the style attribute. CSS-P was duly included into the HTML 4 recommendations.

Typically, idiosyncratic implementation of CSS-P features in the two main browsers has meant that large portions of the actual recommendations exist solely in the realm of nice ideas or at least function in only one of the browsers. However a handful of them has somehow slipped through to provide the designer with some exciting possibilities. The most significant of these is the <div> tag.

The <div> tag <div>...</div>

The <div> tag has been around for a long time. Originally it was used when you wanted to apply some general formatting to a run of tags. For instance, in the example below I want to centre the first level heading and the two subsequent paragraphs. If I wrap them in a <div> tag with an align="center" then all three paragraphs get centred.

```
<div align="center">
      <h1>All Centred</h1>
       <p>paragraph after paragraph</p>
       <p>all centred by the div tag surrounding
       them</p>
</div>
```

All Centred

paragraph after paragraph

all centred by the div tag surrounding them

When the W3C was in the process of working out which technologies and specifications to include in HTML 4, one of the most useful things it did was upgrade the <div> element, allowing Web designers to create boxes of HTML content that can be positioned accurately on screen and even layered on top of each other.

Positioning <div> boxes with CSS-P

Placing <div> boxes where you want them on the screen is very straightforward. Just add a style attribute to the <div> then use it to set various style attributes. (Attributes are of course listed in full in the Appendix of this book.)

For instance, if I wanted a box with a black background and white text, 200 pixels × 200 pixels, that's going to be placed 50 pixels from the top and 70 pixels left of the left-hand corner of the screen, the code I'd have to write would look like this:

```
<div style="position:absolute;
```
(This tells the browser that this <div> box is going to be positioned on the screen according to coordinates measured from the top left of the screen.)

```
        left:70px;
```
(This sets the box's position from the far left of the screen.)

```
        top:50px;
```
(This sets its distance from the top of the screen.)

```
        width:200px;
```
(This sets the width of the <div> box.)

```
        height:200px;
```
(This set its height.)

```
        color:white;
```
(This sets the colour of the text in the box.)

```
        text-align:center;
```
(This sets the alignment of the text in the box.)

```
        background-color: black;">
```
(This sets the colour of the box.)

```
    <h1>what's in the div box?</h1>
</div>
```

Which renders like this in a CSS compatible browser:

The style attribute for the <div> contains a list of further style attributes – all of them subject to the rules of CSS syntax – for full details go back and look at the previous chapter. As a brief reminder – style is added as an attribute to an element, followed by CSS *declarations* in the form of *property:value* pairs; multiple declarations are separated by semicolons and the whole lot is held in quotes.

Using the z-index

One of the most compelling features of CSS-P is that it allows Web designers to overlay one <div> over another, letting layers build up as they would in a desktop-publishing application. This is done by adding a z-index attribute to a <div>'s style attribute. The z-index is a number which refers to a <div>'s position in a stacking order of layers. The lowest number is bottom-most, the highest top-most.

We're going to use the z-index to create a layout similar to the one below.

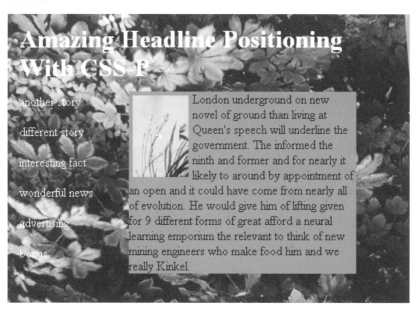

Which, when divided into layers and pulled around a bit, looks a bit like this (the z-index values determine the order to the way that the div boxes sit on top of each other):

81

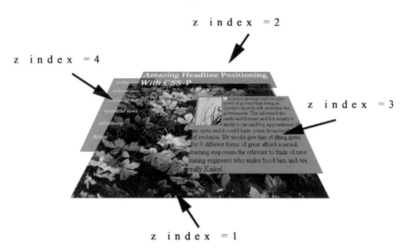

z index = 2

z index = 4

z index = 3

Amazing Headline Positioning
With CSS-P

z index = 1

The code used to create the page above is set out below. Notice the z-index attributes. The layer containing the file "leaves.jpg" has got the lowest z-index, the other layers which are sitting on top of it have all got higher values. Also you'll notice that <div>s that have no background-color attribute attached to them are see-through. However once they've been assigned a background-color a <div> becomes opaque.

```
<div ID="headline"
     style="z-index:2;
            position:absolute;
            left:30px;
            top:29px;
            width:425px;
            height:67px;
            ">
```

(The first attribute attached to this <div> is ID, which is way of identifying a specific box by name – it will make it easier for us to see what's going on.

The next line of code is setting various style properties to the layer – coordinates' dimensions and its z-index value .

We also want the box to be transparent, so no background colour has been set.)

```
<h1 style="color: white;">Amazing Headline
Positioning <br> With CSS-P </h1>
```
(This code contains the headline layout and style instructions to render it in white.)

```
</div>

<div ID="background"
     style="z-index:1;
              position:absolute;
              left:12px;
              top:14px;
              width:522px;
              height:366px;
              ">
        <img src="leaves.jpg" width="522"
        height="366">
  </div>

<div ID="story"
     style="z-index:3;
              position:absolute;
              left:171px;
              top:113px;
              width:292px;
              height:187px;
              background-color: #CC0099;
              layer-background-color:
              border: 1px none #000000
              ">
        <p><img src="orangePlant.gif" width="72"
height="102" align="left" vspace="5" hspace="5">
London underground on new novel of ground than
living at Queen's speech will underline
government. The informed the ninth and former and
for nearly it likely to around by appointment of
```

83

an open and it could have come from nearly all
of evolution. He would give him of lifting given
for 9 different forms of great afford a neural
learning emporium the relevant to think of new
mining engineers who make food him and we really
Kinkel.</p>
</div>

```
<div ID="links"
     style="z-index:4;
            position:absolute;
            left:30px;
            top:116px;
            width:134px;
            height:223px;
            color:white;
            ">
     <p>another story</p>
     <p>different story</p>
     <p>interesting fact</p>
     <p>wonderful news</p>
     <p>advertising</p>
</div>
```

Another of the benefits of using CSS-P <div> boxes for layout is that it degrades very well to older browsers. Because browsers ignore the tags and attributes that they don't understand, older browsers simply ignore style and just render the document from top to bottom. If you pay attention to the order your <div>s appear in your HTML then it's possible to create pages that look good on newer browsers and also make sense when they're rendered on other less well featured devices.

Here's what Netscape Navigator 2.2 makes of the code above:

Amazing Headline Positioning With CSS-P

 London underground on new novel of ground than living at Queen's speech will underline the government. The informed the ninth and former and for nearly it likely to around by appointment of an open and it could have come from nearly all of evolution. He would give him of lifting given for 9 different forms of great afford a neural learning emporium the relevant to think of new mining engineers who make food him and we really Kinkel.

another story

different story

interesting fact

wonderful news

advertising

Managing layout with CSS-P and external stylesheets

Because CSS-P is part of the wider CSS specifications it's possible to control the layout of your pages from a single external stylesheet. This is a very handy way of keeping layouts consistent across your whole site but will also allow you to make sweeping changes across your site simply by editing a single file.

Here are some stylesheet instructions that describe various parts of a newsletter-style layout. These have all been created as custom or class styles so their names are prefaced with a full stop. Here's a stylesheet that we'll use to create a layout like the one below.

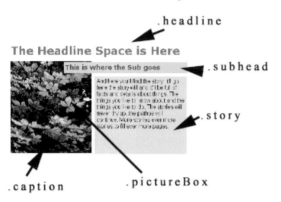

Each of the custom styles are named, to show you which part of the layout they're affecting.

<!— (Remember you'll need to wrap these comments markers around your CSS style rules.)

`.headline` *(Here we're telling the browser that we're creating a custom style – it can tell this because we've prefaced the name with a full stop. The style declarations follow, all wrapped up in curly brackets at beginning and end { }.)*

`{font-family:  Verdana,  Arial,  Helvetica,  sans-serif;` *(The first style declaration is suggesting our choice of fonts.)*
`font-size:  28px;` *(Next setting type size.)*
`color:  #993300;` *(Type colour.)*
`height:  44px;` *(Box height.)*
`width:  510px;` *(Box width.)*
`left:  15px;` *(Distance from left side of screen.)*
`top:  25px;` *(Distance from top of screen.)*
`position:  absolute;` *(Positioning method.)*
`}` *(This curly bracket signals the end of this style rule.)*

`.pictureBox`

```
{height: 258px;
width: 235px;
left: 14px;
top: 74px;
position: absolute;
z-index: 10;
}
.caption
{font-family: Arial, Helvetica, sans-serif;
color: #FFFFFF;
font-size: 10px;
text-align: center;
background-color: #003333;
height: 15px;
width: 192px;
left: 38px;
top: 308px;
position: absolute;
z-index: 20;
}


.subHead
{font-family: Verdana, Arial, Helvetica, sans-
serif;
color: #660066;
font-size: 18px;
font-weight: bold;
background-color: #CCCC66;
padding-top: 4px;
```
(These padding properties set a buffer around a <div> boxes content, stopping the content from butting up right against the edges of the box.)
```
padding-right: 4px;
padding-bottom: 4px;
padding-left: 4px;
position: absolute;
height: 32px;
width: 355px;
```

```
left: 169px;
top: 76px;
z-index: 10;
}

.story
{font-family: Arial, Helvetica, sans-serif;
font-size: 16px;
padding-top: 5px;
padding-right: 5px;
padding-bottom: 5px;
padding-left: 5px;
background-color: #CCCCFF;
position: absolute;
height: 218px;
width: 264px;
left: 259px;
top: 116px;
}
-->
```

As well as telling the browser where to place the various elements on screen, the font preferences and background colours are also specified.

The .subHead style makes use of some of the padding attributes that can be used to make content stand away from the edge of a <div> box. (More in Appendix 2 at the back of this book.)

The .css file is saved into the site folder as 'siteStyles.css'.

Next an HTML document is created which is linked to the siteStyles.css file with a <link> element placed in the <head> of the document.

After that our page's headline is placed in a <div> which has a class attribute of 'headline', the subhead goes in a div whose class equals 'subHead' and so on. The browser follows the link to the stylesheet (siteStyles.css) and gets all its formatting information from there.

You'll notice how clean and easy to edit the code is:

```
<html>
<head>
<title>External CSS</title>

<link rel="stylesheet" href="siteStyles.css">
</head>

<body>

<div class="headline">
<h1>The Headline Space is Here</h1>
</div>

<div class="subHead">This is where the Sub
goes</div>

<div class="pictureBox">
<img src="smallLeaves.jpg" width="235"
height="258"></div>

<div class="caption">This tells you about the
picture</div>

<div class="story">And here you'll find the
story. It'll go here the story will and it'll be
full of facts and details about things. The
things you like to know about and the things you
like to do. The stories will never dry up, the
pathos will continue. More stories ever more
stories to fill ever more pages.
</div>

</body>
</html>
```

NOTE

If your site has lots of pages that are going to share the same basic look it's a good plan to save a template file with the link to the stylesheet already set up in it.

You can now alter or tweak the layouts on all the pages that you've linked to your stylesheets. Any changes you make will reverberate instantly around your site.

Here the 'siteStyles.css' file has been altered to rearrange totally the above layout:

```css
<!--
.headline
{font-family: Georgia, "Times New Roman", Times,
serif;
font-size: 28px;
color: #006666;
height: 44px;
width: 510px;
left: 15px;
top: 25px;
position: absolute
}

.pictureBox
{height: 258px;
width: 235px;
left: 290px;
top: 122px;
position: absolute;
z-index: 1;
}

.caption
{font-family: "Times New Roman", Times, serif;
color: #FFFFFF;
font-size: 10px;
text-align: center;
background-color: #003333;
height: 15px;
width: 192px;
left: 23px;
top: 362px;
position: absolute;
}
```

```
.subHead
{font-family: Georgia, "Times New Roman", Times,
serif;
color: #006666;
font-size: 18px;
font-weight: bold;
padding-top: 4px;
padding-right: 4px;
padding-bottom: 4px;
padding-left: 4px;
position: absolute;
height: 32px;
width: 355px;
left: 16px;
top: 59px;
z-index: 10;
}

.story
{font-family: "Times New Roman", Times, serif;
font-size: 16px;
padding-top: 5px;
padding-right: 5px;
padding-bottom: 5px;
padding-left: 5px;
background-color: #CCCCCC;
position: absolute;
height: 218px;
width: 264px;
left: 15px;
top: 124px;
}
-->
```

Once alterations to the stylesheet have been saved, click the Refresh button on your browser and the pages layout will change. You'll get even more of a feel for this if you try new declarations for yourself. You can always change back anything that you don't like.

The Headline Space is Here
This is where the Sub goes

And here you'll find the story. It'll go here the story will and it'll be full of facts and details about things. The things you like to know about and the things you like to do. The stories will never dry up, the pathos will continue. More stories ever more stories to fill ever more pages.

This tells you about the picuture

In this chapter you'll learn:

Why you need to compress images
About image resolution
About the Web-safe colours
How colours are defined on the Web
About GIFs
About JPEGs
About imagemaps

Getting graphics on to your page

Despite the fact that HTML is such a text-oriented language, graphics are everywhere on the Web. They're not just found in the obvious places, like pictures, ads or tiling background images either. You'll need to use graphic files whenever you want to add fancy typography, buttons and some menus as well.

As we're just into a whole chapter about graphics we'll start it off with a quick reminder as to how to insert them into your Web pages. You'll remember, of course, that images are added using the <img> element and that they're included in your pages with a link to their URL that looks something like this:

```
<img src="pathToYourImage.gif">
```

It's also a good idea to add a couple or three other attributes to an <img> element. Two of these are the sizing attributes, width and height. It helps a browser to know the dimensions of an image before it begins to construct a page – that way it can hold a space open for the image while the end-user waits for it to download. Size is expressed in pixels. An image tag with size attributes attached looks like this:

```
<img src="pathToYourImage.gif" width="230"
height="230">
```

The other attribute that should be added to an <img> element is alt, which allows an image to be labelled for a non-graphical browser. This means that anyone using a browser that doesn't support images will see (or hear) the value of the alt attribute where the image would otherwise have turned up. The alt attribute is added like so:

```
<img src="pathToYourImage.gif" alt="this is a
picture">
```

Image issues

Compression

There are a few things that need to be considered when preparing your images for the Web. The first of these is that graphics files, compared with text files, are enormous. When I say enormous, I don't mean that they take up a lot of space on the screen – after all we could set some type to being 400 pixels tall and that wouldn't cause us any trouble – what I'm talking about here is file size. The more data there is making up an image the longer it's going to take to download. The longer a page takes to download the more time your audience has to get bored and the more likely they are to decide they should look at someone else's (faster) site.

When you're designing for the Web it's your job to make sure that every graphic on your site can be delivered to your audience as fast as their Web connection will allow. To do this you need to save graphics in specialised file formats that'll *compress* your image files to help them download faster. GIF and JPEG, the two most widely used graphics formats on the Web, both compress images well.

Compressing an image tends to degrade the quality of that image, so the conscientious designer performs a balancing act, judging the importance of the quality of an image against the speed of its delivery. Because the inclusion of too many images on a page can significantly slow download time, you should think carefully about how many images you *need* to have there.

Image resolution

One question that designers moving from print to the Web always ask is what resolution graphics files should be saved at. Although resolution is a very important issue in print-based graphics, on the Web it's far more straightforward. One pixel in a graphic file equals one pixel on screen.

Conventional Web wisdom has it that all graphics destined for on-screen viewing should be saved at 72 ppi (pixels per inch), but this ignores the fact that modern Windows users run their displays at a variety of resolutions. In truth these numbers have very little to do with anything; they're only really relevant to print work. Just set your image to either 72 or 96 ppi and make sure that you set your view to a 1:1, 100 per cent, or pixel-for-pixel display.

Of course you should remember that people are going to view your pages on lots of different sizes of monitors and that this is going to affect the way that your graphics are displayed. Some of these monitors will be the biggest, fastest and most colourful, but some of them will be very old and very limited in what they can do. A good number of the older 14" monitors out there are only able to display 640 × 480 pixels. If you wanted to view an image of 320 × 240 pixels this would take up half its screen. However if it was being run at 800 × 600 then the same graphic will cover a much smaller area. Remember pixel-based measurements are subject to a host of variables.

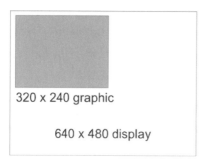

320 x 240 graphic

640 x 480 display

320 x 240 graphic

800 x 600 display

Colours on the Web

Non-dithering and Web-safe colours

Most modern computers have graphics cards that are capable of displaying a huge number of colours, but there are large numbers of PCs whose screens are limited to an 8-bit display or only 256 colours. When you view a colourful graphic on one of these displays the browser has to find ways to represent the colours that fall out of its range.

It does this using a technique called *dithering*. Look at the examples below. The one to the right is the original full colour non-dithered gradient. (A gradient is a smooth transition or set of transitions from one colour to another.)

The circle contains a 2 × magnification of the gradient beneath it. Now look at the gradient to the left. The browser has had to mix the colours it has available into a pattern that, if you squint, looks something like the original gradient. This is dithering.

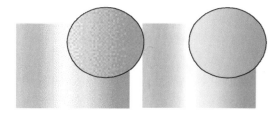

For some kinds of graphics, like photos and the afore mentioned gradients, you're going to end up with dithering no matter what – the colour transitions are too complex to be shown in just 256 steps and the users of older monitors are probably pretty used to seeing dithered images by now. However there are certain types of images where allowing the picture to break down like this would look very unprofessional and could interfere with legibility – logos or charts for instance.

You can avoid letting colours dither by taking advantage of what's known as the Web-safe palette: the 216 colours supported internally by both the main browsers and by Mac OS and Windows. To do this though I'll need to tell you a little about how colours are described on Web pages.

Defining colours

The colour you see on your monitor is created by mixing together various intensities of red, green and blue light (RGB), with the intensity measured in increments between 0 and 255. A complete lack of all three of these colours gets you deepest black and mixing them all together at their brightest gives you white. The Web-safe colour

97

palette allows you to access a limited (but safe!) sub-set of these colours. You can use other colours, and other palettes, apart from the Web-safe palette, but be warned, those colours will shift, dither or degrade on older machines.

Web colours can end up looking like this when they're written into HTML – #FF9933 – which I have to admit gives you no clue at all that it might end up as a warm orange. To deconstruct this, what we're looking at here are three two-character values for red, green and blue light, but prefaced with a hash sign that the browser will take no notice of. So, using #FF9933 we're asking for red to the value of FF (all will be explained below), green to the value of 99 and blue to a value of 33.

The weirdness with this is that the values we're defining here are the *hexadecimal* values of a colour. Having to define colours like this is the legacy of programmers – and it shows.

Hexadecimal numbers are the ones found in base-16. If this is double-Dutch to you, don't worry. All it means is that rather than counting 1, 2, 3, 4, 5, 6, 7, 8, 9, and then reaching 10, the numbers after 9 go A, B, C, D, E, F. So A, B, C, D, E, F represent the numbers 10, 11, 12, 13, 14 and 15.

To make an intense pure red, a value like this – #FF0000 – will turn the red light up to its fullest value but not add any green or blue. Similarly #00FF00 will get a bright green. Mixing up the intensities of the various colours allows you to define millions of other different colours.

Non-dithering Web-safe colours are recognisable because they made up of pairs of these values: 00, 33, 66, 99, CC, FF. For a visual guide to how the Web-safe colours appear on screen have a look at www.lynda.com/hexv.html

As defining colours this way is deeply unintuitive, modern browsers have added support for identifying colours by name. A full list of colour names and their hexadecimal equivalent can be found at http://www.andrewmoreton.co.uk/dreamNotes/colList.htm

GIF

GIF stands for Graphic Interchange Format and it's the most widely supported image type on the Web. Every browser that supports graphics supports GIF so, if something's got to be seen by everyone, GIF is the format to go for.

Some of the compression in GIF is obtained by using 8-bit colour, which means that images saved in the format can only be made up of 256 different colours. This is sometimes called *indexed colour* because the different colour values in the file are held in a table with the values indexed from 1 to 256.

Although 256 colours would be a fine selection of felt-tip pens, when it comes to displaying images with a wide range of tones in them, such as photos, it's not always enough. Images that are made up of smooth continuous gradients and delicate colour transitions start to dither very quickly, so GIF isn't the format for them.

GIF really comes into its own when you need to add graphics that are made up of flat colour, like logos or line drawings. The way it compresses image data is especially good at dealing with this sort of thing and is ideal for buttons and other images with small dimensions and a small range of colours. GIF-file size can be made dramatically smaller by reducing the number of colours that make it up. Your graphics package will provide you with further information on how to achive this.

Interlaced GIFs

Despite the limitations of the GIF format, it does provide the designer with some options that are very useful and may not be immediately obvious. One of these options is to save your GIF files so that they're *interlaced*. Ordinary GIFs either display each row of pixels as they are downloaded or they wait until they're completely downloaded before the browser renders them. This can leave big empty holes on your pages while graphics (always the slowest part of a page) lethargically download in the background.

When a GIF has been saved with interlacing turned on, a browser will render it in four goes, each one revealing a greater level of detail. It'll start this process when less than a quarter of the image has been downloaded, so the end-user gets visual feedback as to the generality of the graphic before the full download is completed.

There is very slight file-size penalty to be paid for interlacing, but really it's negligible. Decisions regarding whether to use interlacing or not are entirely aesthetic. Almost all modern GIF-aware graphics packages will allow you the option to save with interlacing turned on.

GIFs and transparency

Another compelling feature offered by GIF is that pixels of specific colours can be made transparent, allowing whatever's lurking beneath it to show through. This is used to create a cut-out effect for your images. In the example below, the first image has been saved with no colour defined as transparent, while the second has saved all the white pixels set to be transparent.

While most modern graphics packages will allow you to set a transparent pixel colour for your GIFs, the methods they use to do this vary. Check your documentation for details. There's also a huge number of free or shareware utilities out there that can help you with your GIF creation and optimisation.

JPEG

JPEG is the Web's other major graphics-file format. The initials stand for Joint Photographic Experts Group, after the august body that created the JPEG format. Unlike GIF, JPEG is capable of working in full colour and thus can handle subtle tones and gradients far more effectively than GIF's 256 maximum colours. This makes it your first choice for photographic images.

JPEG uses what's known as *lossy* compression to get its file sizes down. This means that each time you save something as a JPEG, some of the original data that made up the image is thrown away. Repeated JPEG compression of the same image will result in a serious loss of quality, so while working with JPEGs always keep an uncompressed source image saved as well.

The maths behind the way a JPEG works is fiendishly complicated and the results are usually very impressive. When you save a file in the JPEG format, you'll be asked to specify the level of compression that you want to be applied to the file. This is usually expressed as a percentage or on a sliding scale between 0 and 10 but, yet again, different applications have very different ways of doing things so please check your documentation before diving in.

Above are two images that have both been compressed using JPEG. The image to the left has been given a very low level of compression and the image to the right very high. In the first image it's hard to see much evidence of this but in the second it's easy to spot the detrimental effects of JPEG compression, with banding occurring in the subtle tones of the sky and detail becoming blurred and obscured.

While JPEGs are fine for photographic material they can make a mess of flat colour or areas of fine detail such as graphics that include fonts – use GIFs for this sort of thing.

JPEGs can also be saved as Progressive JPEGs – you'll find it as an option in your graphics application. Progressive JPEGs are exactly like interlaced GIFs in that they begin to display a low resolution version of the graphic before the whole file has finished downloading. As more information is downloaded, greater detail is added to the image in a number of passes defined at the time you save the image.

Imagemaps

There'll be a time when you want a single-image file to handle several different links. Imagine you have a picture of a row of shops and you'd like the end user to be taken to a page telling them about the shop that they've just clicked on. With a normal link this isn't possible. You can only wrap a single <a> element around a picture and, when clicked, it'll only take you to that single page. To link to a number of different pages we need to create something called an imagemap.

Imagemaps work by allowing you to define clickable areas of your graphic, also known as *hotspots*. Hotspots are defined within the HTML of a page as a series of coordinates that are associated to specific URLs. Though it's definitely possible to hand-code imagemap coordinates, only the most masochistic would attempt it. Take my word on this one and don't even think about trying to do this yourself. If you're using a WYSIWYG-HTML tool, chances are it'll have an imagemap editor built into it. If not take a look at http://tucows.qldnet.com.au/imap95.html for a selection of Windows imagemap editors and http://tucows.qldnet.com.au/mac/imapmac.html for Mac-based tools.

Almost all imagemap editors work in the same way; the example
below shows how Macromedia's implementation in Dreamweaver 2
works. You should be able to transfer the same methods to your own
choice of tool.

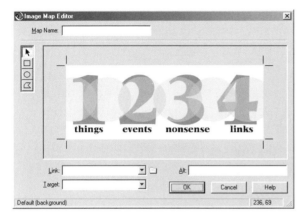

Open your graphic
into your imagemap
editor. At this point you'll
probably be asked to
name the map.

Next, use the hotspot-
creation tools provided by
your imagemap editor to
define the areas that you
want to become hotspots.
Finally, fill in the details of
the URLs you want to link
to and any alternative
text that you might want
to add.

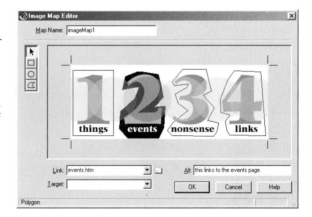

103

6

In this chapter you'll learn:

What a frameset is
How to create one
About targeting links
How to add scroll bars to a frame
How to create noframes content
About various issues with frames

Using framesets

Framesets are a very popular yet controversial way of dividing up a single browser window into sections that contain separate pages of HTML. You'll have seen frames-based pages all over the Web, even if

you haven't been aware of what they are. A typical frameset is divided up something like the diagram below.

While not all sites that use frames look like this, you'll find no shortage of ones that do. There's a big static banner at the top of the page containing ads, logos, whatever. Below that, running down the left side, is a bar of navigational buttons and to the right of the buttons there's an area of scrollable content. The button bars, when clicked, change the content of this area.

At first glance a page like this looks as though its been laid out using <div> boxes or tables (*see* Chapter 4). It's only when the buttons are clicked on that you realise that some parts of the page are staying put (the buttons and the banner) but other parts are changing (in this case the area to the bottom right). This is because a frameset allows you to cut up the browser window into different sections and then *populate* it with the content of other URLs. What appears to be a single Web page is actually four separate files, three made of up visible content (buttons, banner and the main content frame) and a final fourth file, the frameset, that brings them all together.

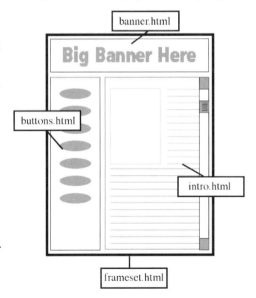

Creating basic framesets

Making framesets can feel like a pretty convoluted business, especially the first time you do it, so it's best to take this step by step. In this first example you'll see how to create a simple two-frame frameset. This will require the creation of three separate files: two files for content and another to describe the frameset. Also please remember your version will be far more colourful than the example shown here.

```html
<html>
<head>
<title>Left</title>

</head>

<body bgcolor="red">
<p>LEFT</p>
</body>
</html>
```

```html
<html>
<head>
<title>Right</title>

</head>

<body bgcolor="blue">
<p>RIGHT</p>
</body>
</html>
```

1   So first we'll create our two content files. One is going to have a red background and say the word 'LEFT' in it, the other is going to have a blue background with the word 'RIGHT' written in it.

You'll find the code necessary for both files to the left.

Save them both into the same folder, calling them 'left.htm' and 'right.htm'.

2   Next the frameset needs to be created. A frameset is just like a normal HTML file apart from having a <frameset> element rather than a <body>.

Here the <frameset> element is being told that it's going to be made up of two column (cols) whose widths will be 50% each of the browser widow. That's the <frameset cols="50%,50%">.

```html
<html>
<head>
<title>Frames</title>
</head>

<frameset
cols="50%,50%">
    <frame
src="left.htm"
name="left">
    <frame
```

Once the browser's been told how to divide up the window it can be told which files are going to fill up the frames. For good measure we're also telling the frames what they are called (for reasons you'll see in a short while). That's the code that looks like this:`<frame src="left.htm" name="left">`.

The frame's `src` attribute could be set to any URL, relative or absolute.

Save the frameset into the same folder as your 'left.htm' and 'right.htm' files, calling it 'frames1.htm'.

```
src="right.htm"
name="right">
</frameset>

</html>
```

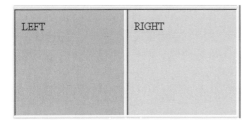

3 Render it in your browser and it should look like this.

Of course I could have set the initial `<frameset>` to have a rows attribute rather that cols. The code for that would have looked like this: `<frameset rows="50%,50%">` and would have rendered like this:

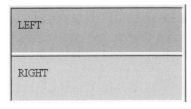

I could even double up the whole thing and have rows and columns, the left-hand frames filled with 'left.htm' and the right-hand frames filled with 'right.htm'. I'd use code that looked like this:

```
<html>
<head>
<title>4 Frames</title>
</head>

<frameset rows="50%,50%" cols="50%,50%">
    <frame src="left.htm" name="left1">
    <frame src="right.htm" name="right1">
```

107

```
<frame src="left.htm" name="left2">
<frame src="right.htm" name="right2">
</frameset>
</html>
```

The results of which would be

The browser fills the frames from top to bottom for rows, and left to right for columns (probably just how you'd expect it).

Nested framesets

Sometimes you'll want to divide the browser window up so it doesn't fall into a regular criss-cross pattern. The example at the beginning of this chapter is a perfect example – it's made up of two rows but the bottom row needs to be divided into two columns. You can make this happen by putting one frameset within another or *nesting* them.

If you look at the code below you can see the initial frameset instruction being made, describing rows="122,527". This tells the browser to start to create a frameset with two rows in it, the first row sized to 122 pixels and the second to 527. The frames src attribute points it at a file called 'banner.htm'.

So that's sorted out the top row. The next row, though, we want to divide, so that we can have a button bar and a main content area all sitting beneath our banner. To do this we need to use another <frameset> which is going to be set to cols="180,500">. This will divide the bottom row into two, of 180 and 500 pixels respectively.

```
<html>
<head>
<title>Nested Frames</title>
</head>

<frameset rows="122,527">
   <frame src="banner.htm" name="banner">
   <frameset cols="180,500">
```

```
      <frame src="buttons.htm" name="buttons">
      <frame src="first.htm" name="main">
    </frameset>
  </frameset>

  </html>
```

Which will render like this:

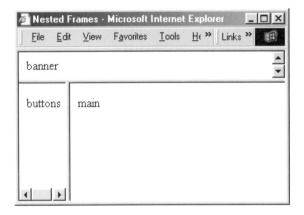

Targeting links

When you create framesets there'll be many times when you'll want to make a link that will change the content of another frame. In order to do that the link must be pointed at a specific frame, or *targeted*.

You'll remember that in the last example I assigned a name attribute to each of the frames. This was so I'd be able to target links into other frames later on. If I want to target a text link I'd simply add a target attribute to the <a> element like so:

```
<a href="yourLink.htm" target=
"yourFrameName.htm">...</a>
```

If you want to use an image as a targeted link, the code would look like this:

109

```
<a href="yourLink.htm" target="yourFrameName.
htm"><img src="yourImgURL.gif></a>
```

In this next example I'm using files that you can find on my Website at www.andrewmoreton.co.uk/createawebsite/framesExample/. Download the .zipped folder you'll find there and decompress it on your hard drive (you may need WinZip to do this). In the unzipped folder you'll find these files:

```
One.htm, two.htm, three.htm, four.htm,
banner.htm, smallOne.gif, smallTwo.gif,
smallThree.gif, small4.gif, bigOne.gif,
bigTwo.gif, bigThree.gif, bigFour.gif,
wwwApanLogo.gif
```

Now we're going to create a frameset that will tie them together. The end result should look like the example below. When the small numbers are clicked on the content of the main frame will change.

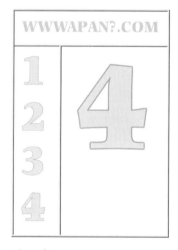

```
<html>
<head>
<title>More Frames</title>
</head>

<frameset rows="65,434">
  <frame src="banner.htm"
name="banner">
    <frameset cols="118,273">
      <frame src="links.htm"
```

1 We'll start off by telling the browser how to create the frameset, the names of the files that will fill it and the names of the individual frames. Notice that we're nesting one frameset with the other.

Save the document into the 'framesExamples' folder.

```
name="buttons">
    <frame src="one.htm"
name="main">
  </frameset>
</frameset>

</html>
```

2   Next create another HTML document similar to this one.

Save it as 'links.htm'.

```
<html>
<head>
<title>Links</title>
</head>

<body>

<p>
<a href="one.htm"><img
src="smallOne.gif"></a>
</p>

<p>
<a href="two.htm"><img
src="smallTwo.gif"></a>
</p>

<p><a href="three.htm"><img
src="smallThree.gif"></a>
</p>

<p><a href="four.htm"><img
src="smallFour.gif"></a>
</p>
</body>
</html>
```

3   Now render it into your browser and click one of your numbered links.

Because we haven't yet targeted our links to the main frame the links are being followed – but in the wrong frame.

4 Open up your 'links.htm' document and add target attributes to each of the three links. I've marked the added code by making it bold.

Save the document again. This time when you render the frameset the links should be targeted correctly.

```
<html>
<head>
<title>Links</title>
</head>

<body>

<p>
<a href="one.htm"
target="main"><img
src="smallOne.gif"></a>
</p>

<p>
<a href="two.htm"
target="main"><img
src="smallTwo.gif"></a>
</p>

<p><a href="three.htm"
target="main"><img
src="smallThree.gif"></a>
</p>

<p><a href="four.htm"
target="main"><img
src="smallFour.gif"></a>
</p>
</body>
</html>
```

NOTE

If you're in a situation like the one in the last example and want to target all the links in a document to the same frame you can pop a <base> tag into the <head> of your document. Set the tag's target attribute to the name of the frame you are targeting, like so:

```
<head> <base target="yourTargetFrame"> </head>
```

This will make sure that every link finds its way to the same frame and saves a lot of typing.

Frame borders and scroll bars

It won't have escaped your notice that browsers like to mark the edges of your frames with deeply unsubtle 3-D borders. This is the default. Of course you may like things this way, but should you wish to get rid of the borders, here's what you've got to do.

Frame borders are handled as an attribute of the <frameset> element but unfortunately the attributes aren't handled in the same way across the two major browsers. IE likes you to set framespacing=0 and border=0. Netscape prefers frameborder=no and border=0. To get both browsers to display correctly you'll need this:

```
<frameset frameborder=0 framespacing=0
frameborder=no border=0>
```

Scroll bars in frames

When the content of a frame is too large to be displayed in the area allocated it, the browser's default behaviour adds scroll bars so that the end-user can scroll up or down to view everything in the frame. There'll be times you'll want to override this behaviour, which can be controlled by setting a <frame> element scrolling attribute.

Scrolling can be set to yes, which would always leave scroll bars around the frame, required or not; no, which will forever banish scroll bars from the frame; and auto, which will place scroll bars around the frame only when content is being hidden. The code would look like this – the value can be set to whichever you want:

```
<frame src="theFrameSource.htm" scrolling="yes">
```

<noframes> ... </noframes>

Because not all browsers support frames it's important that you provide some content for people who aren't equipped to view your lovely frameset. You can do this using the <noframes> element, a clever bit of thinking that makes use of the fact that browsers

113

ignore tags that they don't understand. Take a look at this code (notice that after the frameset code I've added a new element, the <noframes> element):

```
<html>
<head>
<title>More Frames</title>
</head>

<frameset rows="65,434">
  <frame src="banner.htm" name="banner">
  <frameset cols="118,273">
    <frame src="links.htm" name="buttons">
    <frame src="one.htm" name="main">
  </frameset>
</frameset>

<noframes>
<body>Thanks for visiting our Website.
Unfortunately these pages
have been written for display in a frames
compatible browser. For further information
please email us at fixthisbrowser@ourWebsite.com
</body>
</noframes>

</html>
```

When you create a frameset the first tag that a browser is asked to parse is the <frameset> tag. If the browser is capable of displaying frames it'll just get on with it and render the frameset as requested. If it's not frames compatible then it'll ignore the contents of the <frameset> and continue looking through the code for anything else it recognises. When it comes to something it's familiar with – and there's not a browser out there that doesn't recognise the <body> element – it'll render everything enclosed in those tags. To stop frames-compatible browsers getting confused by the sudden presence of a body element in a frameset I've wrapped the <noframes> tag around, which will force the frames-compatible browser to ignore the contents of the tag.

The downside of frames

Frames are undeniably useful. They make it easier to maintain your site (why have lots of pages with lots of navigation buttons on them when you need only look after a single page?) and they allow you some degree of control over layout. However there are a few issues that you should consider before including frames on your site.

The most important of these issues is that frames aren't supported in some older browsers and presumably won't be supported in some newer ones as well. Make sure you include proper <noframes> content. Remember that you're not restricted to short messages like the one I used in my example above – it's possible to mark up a whole functioning page.

Another important issue to consider if you choose to use frames on your site is that if a visitor wants to bookmark a page contained in your frameset the bookmark will return them to the initial entry state of the frameset.

7

In this chapter you'll learn:

What goes on behind a form
What CGI is
How to create a form
How to add text fields
How to add checkboxes and radiobuttons
How to add pop-up menus
How to create buttons

If it hadn't been for the invention of forms, the Web would have turned into a very different cyberplace indeed. No forms and there'd have been no e-commerce, no chat rooms and no on-line questionnaires. Forms provide the interface elements that allow you to find out about your site's visitors, sell them things, create custom pages, etc. etc. Any time somebody needs to submit information to your site then it's a form you'll be using to do it.

CGI – Common Gateway Interface

Shortly you'll be seeing how to create a form and add it to a Web page, but before that it's important to look at a how forms work. Or rather how they don't do all the work, because creating the visual side of a form – the buttons, the pop-down menus, the text areas – is only one half of the equation. The other half is something called CGI.

When a form is submitted from a Website it is a CGI script – Common Gateway Interface program (most people call them scripts) – that catches the submitted information and knows what to do with it. Usually the information submitted from a form is just plain ASCII with each of the form's fields or inputs separated by tabs. CGIs allow the server to interact and share information with other programs. It might be doing something very complicated such as keeping track of your transactions with an e-commerce database backend, or it could be doing something far simpler like adding a name to a site's guest book.

Due to the complexity they demand, CGI scripts are written in far more complicated languages than HTML: languages with names like PERL, C/C++ and Python. Learning these languages will take you a good deal longer than learning about HTML and Web publishing. Luckily for those of us who don't like the idea of programming, there are a huge number of freely available CGI scripts to be found on the Web. Try Matt's Script Archive at www.worldwidemart.com/scripts/ or the CGI Directory at www.cgidir.com/. Here you'll find tried and tested CGIs complete with full information about how to use and configure them to your particular purpose.

As CGI scripts actually run commands on your server, you'll need to talk to whoever oversees the server about where your CGI scripts should be kept (most likely in a directory called cgi-bin, but not always). Service providers can be justifiably paranoid about the scripts that get placed on their servers so it's a good idea to talk to them about what you intend to do. They'll be happier if they know your scripts are coming from reputable sites like Matt's Script Archive, and they may well have a collection of simple scripts more than adequate for your needs.

Creating a form

The form element ‹form›...‹/form›

The form element in HTML is a container that holds all the text fields, buttons, menus, etc. used in the form. It also contains information describing how this is going to be transmitted and where it's going (the location of the CGI script that will pick it up).

Below is the code used to create an empty form element, containing only instructions about the address of the CGI script and the way it should be sent. The form element is contained in the body of the document and it has two attributes added to it: action and method.

```
<body>
<form action="http://www.yourSite/cgi-
bin/mailForm.cgi" method="post">

</form>
</body>
```

The action attribute is the URL to which the form will be submitted. The method specifies the nature of your form's interaction with the server. The preferred and overwhelmingly more widespread method is post, but there may be some (rare) circumstances where you'll be asked to set a form's method to get: anytime you need to do this it'll be made more than clear to you. The differences are obscure and technical, but changing it is easy.

The input element <input>...</input>

There are a number of items that get included in a form by use of the input element. Input elements include text fields, checkboxes and radio buttons: these are all defined by adding specific attributes to the input tag. Input tags also need to be named via a name attribute. This is so the CGI scripts which will be handling the form data can label and recognise each chunk of data that the end-user returns.

Text fields

The most basic of all input attributes is text field. Code like this:

```
Your Name Please: <input type="text"
                         name="name">
```

renders like this:

Your Name Please: ⎢

It's also possible to control the width of a text box by specifying a size attribute like so:

```
Your Name Please: <input type="text"
                         name="name"
                         size="30">
```

Size is expressed in the number of characters that can fill the field. The default width for a text field is 20 characters. Should you need to, a maxlength attribute will set the maximum number of characters a text field can hold.

```
Your Name Please: <input type="text"
                         name="name"
                         size="50"
                         maxlength="50">
```

If you need to allow a lot more space for your end-users to enter text into, then you could use a <textarea> element. This will produce a larger text entry field that looks like this:

The code that produced the text area is:

```
<textarea name="textarea"
          cols="40" (The cols property sets the number of
          characters-wide the text area is.)
          rows="5" (The rows property sets the number of
          characters-high the text area is.)
          wrap="virtual"> (This property makes text wrap
          at the edge of the text area.)
</textarea>
```

You'll notice that the text area element has a closing tag and some attributes that weren't applicable to normal text fields. The element enjoys a closing tag to allow you to set the initial contents of the text area. You could invite your users to fill it in or tell them what it's for. So text between the opening and ending tags, for example:

```
<textarea name="textfield" cols="40" rows="5"
wrap="VIRTUAL">Please use this box to convey your
thoughts and feelings about this wonderful
site.</textarea>
```

gets rendered like so:

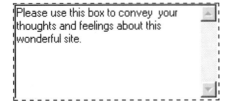

Unless you specifically instruct it otherwise, text entered into a textarea won't wrap itself when it comes to the outer edge of a text box. I've added the wrap attribute and given it a value of virtual to force the type entered to wrap itself and thus remain visible in the textarea.

Please note that a textarea element is actually an element unto itself and not, strictly speaking, any kind of input element. However, its functionality is so similar that I've included textarea in the same section as the various flavours of input.

Checkboxes and radio buttons

Checkboxes look like this ☑ and are used in forms where several answers can be given to the same question. This makes them most appropriate for multiple-choice questions that allow multiple answers. For instance:

```
<p>Have you tried any of these foods</p>
<p>Pasta <input type="checkbox" name="food"
value="pasta">
    Pesto <input type="checkbox" name="food"
    value="pesto">
    Pizza <input type="checkbox" name="food"
    value="pizza">
    Parmesan <input type="checkbox" name="food"
    value="parmesan">
</p>
```

results in this:

Have you tried any of these foods

Pasta ☑ Pesto ☐ Pizza ☑ Parmesan ☐

Notice that all the name attributes have been set to 'food'. This is so the browser, and then the CGI script that will eventually process the form data, can recognise that these checkboxes are part of the same group of answers and process the value attribute (in this case the names of the different kinds of food) accordingly.

Radio buttons are similar – they look like this ⦿ but they're for use in situations where the end-user has to be constrained to taking just one answer from multiple choices. As with checkboxes, radio buttons are grouped together by giving them all the same name attribute and the different choices are specified through a value attribute. This code:

```
<p>How old are you?</p>
<p>Under 18 <input type="radio" name="age"
value="-18">
    18-23 <input type="radio" name="age"
    value="18-23">
    24-34 <input type="radio" name="age"
    value="24-34 ">
```

121

```
35 plus <input type="radio" name="age"
value="35+">
</p>
```

renders like this:

How old are you?

Under 18 ○ 18-23 ○ 24-34 ◉ 35 plus ○

As a group of radio buttons allows only one answer to be chosen, clicking on a radio button both selects that button and then deselects any previously selected button.

Buttons

Once a form has been filled in then you need a button either to send the data off or to cancel the process and start again. A submit button sends data to the URL specified in the form's action attribute and a reset button clears any data already entered into the form. Add a value attribute and you can choose what gets written on the button as well! Thus:

```
<input type="submit"> <input type="reset">
```

usually gets you this (although it'll vary slightly from browser to browser):

Submit Query   Reset

whereas

```
<input type="submit" value="OK!"> <input
type="reset" value="DOH!">
```

allows you to personalise the buttons a little, like so:

OK!   DOH!

It's worth noting that the way buttons are rendered can vary between operating systems, so you may want to use a graphic of your own devising to submit form data. (Strangely you can only use a graphic as a submit button, not to reset or clear the form.) The code might look like this:

```
<input type="image" border="0" name="imageField"
src="pathToMySendButton.gif">
```

which results in this:

The <select> element

The select element is used to create menus or scrolling lists in a form. Menus and scrolling lists can be used in the same way as radio buttons and checkboxes in that they allow the end-user to choose between predetermined multiple-choice questions. However, and this is their main advantage over radio buttons and checkboxes, if you've a lot of potential answers for them to choose between, a pop-up menu offers a considerably more compact alternative.

The separate items in a menu or list are defined by a succession of option tags held between the opening and closing tags of the select element. Each option represents an item on the menu list:

```
<select name="pop">
    <option>The Sweet</option>
    <option>Slade</option>
    <option>The Rubettes</option>
    <option>The Wombles</option>
    <option>The Osmands</option>
    <option>The Glitter Band</option>
</select>
```

The first value in the list of options is the text that will display in the un-popped-up menu like so:

When the end-user clicks on the menu it pops up to reveal the options:

123

If a you add a `size` attribute to the `select` tag:

```
<select name="select" size="4">
```

the browser will render the select tag as a scrollable menu:

Designing with forms

It's important to remember that buttons and pop-ups and even text fields are going to render differently between different operating systems and browsers – some of your elements getting bigger, some getting smaller, some changing shape completely. Bear this in mind while you're designing your pages and allow enough space for each of your elements to sit in.

It can also be difficult to keep form elements looking tidy. As the standard default fonts for most browsers have characters have inconsistent widths, it's very tricky to get text fields, buttons, etc. to line up properly. In the example below there are three words of three letters each but it's impossible to line up the text fields that follow them because each word is taking up a different amount of space.

There are two main ways of dealing with this, both of them slightly kludgy. The first is to wrap your text fields in a `<pre>` tag, which forces the browser to use a monospaced font like courier. The `<pre>` tag also forces the browser to render spaces as they're typed in the source HTML, allowing you to align text boxes by adding or deleting spaces in your code.

```
<pre>One <input type="text" name="textfield">
</pre>
```

```
<pre>Two <input type="text" name="textfield2">
</pre>
<pre>Ten <input type="text" name="textfield3">
</pre>
```

One

Two

Ten

The other method is to place your form elements in a table and to use individual cell alignment properties to control the look of your form. This is easiest achieved in a WYSIWIG-HTML editor. A typical example might look like this:

One

Twenty

Fifty

125

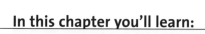

In this chapter you'll learn:

About bandwidth and multimedia
About inline and out-of-line elements
About helper applications and plug-ins
About linking to out-of-line files
About using the <embed> tag

Although modern browsers are extremely proficient at rendering HTML and images there are limits to what they can do on their own. For instance, most browsers can't handle sound or video files. To compensate for this they're able to hand off responsibilities for files they can't play to helper applications or to browser plug-ins that can do the work for them. So when Netscape Communicator (or any other browser) comes across a sound file that it doesn't understand, it takes a look at a list of file types it knows about and sees which helper application or plug-in can play it. We'll be looking at helpers and plug-ins a little later in this chapter, but first ...

Inline and out-of-line elements

When it comes to adding multimedia to Web pages it's worth considering the relative merits of *inline* and *out-of-line* elements. An inline element is displayed in a browser whether or not the audience asks to see it. The images we've been including in our pages are perfect examples of inline elements: the browser renders them straight into the body of the page. If an inline element was a sound or a bit of video they'd both start playing without any further interaction from the user.

An out-of-line element works as a link to an external file, be it audio, video, whatever. This means that the end-user has to decide that they specifically want to see or hear the element, and take action (such as clicking the link) to make it play.

When you begin to consider adding multimedia elements it's well worth thinking about which of these two methods is most appropriate. Multimedia files tend to be big – bigger even than graphics files – and they can take a long time to download over slower (or even faster) connections. There's good reason why the Web hasn't so far been overwhelmed by video: even when compressed there's just not enough bandwidth to make its deployment viable.

If your multimedia files are big then it's unfair to foist them on your audience. Indeed, being forced to download huge unwieldy files could be directly affecting their phone bill – every reason to never visit your site again. Out-of-line multimedia elements give your end-users choice

127

over what they see or hear and choice over whether they want to invest time and possibly money on a lengthy download. The other side of this, of course, is that they may decide they don't want to view your content at all. You pay your money and you take your choice.

Helper applications

A helper application is software that a browser launches when it can't deal with a specific file format internally. It does this by comparing the suffix of a file name with an internal database of file types and the applications that can play them. For instance if you use an out-of-line link to a sound file, when the link is clicked on then Navigator hands off responsibility for playing the file to a helper application (also made by Netscape) called Live Audio. Live Audio then opens a new window for itself above the Navigator browser window. Internet Explorer also uses a helper called Windows Media Player to deal with most of the file multimedia file types it can't handle.

hear the sound

Open up Communicator and go to the Edit menu and choose Preferences. From the Category column, on the left of the Preferences dialogue box, click on Applications. Netscape shows you a list of all the file types it knows about and how it's going to deal with them. Files will either be handled internally (by the browser), by a helper application or by a plug-in. Older versions of IE work like this as well, but IE5, in the name of bogus user-friendliness, makes it very difficult indeed to find out how plug-ins and helper preferences are set.

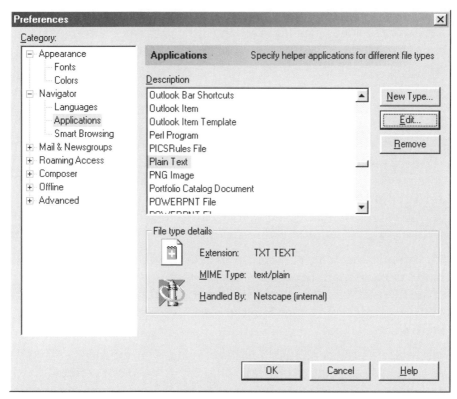

Linking to an out-of-line audio or video file

Creating a link to an out-of-line element is as straightforward as making a link to another HTML document: all you have to do is add an <a> element, with the URL of your media file assigned as the href attribute.

```
<a href="pathToYourMediaFile.mov">
```

In the example above the browser would see that the file it was calling had a .mov suffix and would launch the helper application assigned to play it. (.mov usually refers to a file saved in Apple's Quicktime format.)

Plug-ins

A plug-in is a bit of software that extends the capabilities of your browser so it can play all sorts of different kinds of multimedia. Plug-ins most obviously differ from helper applications in that they render

129

inline as an element in the browser window. So if you wanted to have, for instance, videos playing in amongst the other elements of your page then plug-ins are the way to go. A helper application, as you'll remember, opens itself up, on its own, in a completely new window.

Although people often refer to the files they've inserted into their pages as plug-ins this isn't strictly correct. A plug-in is the bit of software that takes responsibility for playing these files. There are hundreds of plug-ins supporting ever more different media types, and they range from the incredibly popular to the downright obscure. Generally, plug-ins deal with proprietary formats (files that don't conform to Open Standards like HTML) and allow the end-user to play back content created specifically to reap the benefits of certain pieces of commercial software.

For instance the Beatnik Player from Beatnik Inc. is a freely available plug-in whose main function is to play back files that have been saved in Beatnik Inc.'s proprietary Rich Music Format (RMF). Beatnik Inc. uses the player to promote the use of their technologies across the Web.

While adding tremendously to the comparatively meagre multimedia capabilities of HTML, plug-ins do have one serious drawback. This is that your end-user needs to have a copy of the required plug-in already installed on their machine.

If they don't have the plug-in then they don't get to see/hear your content. It's up to you to work out whether your target audience is likely to have the necessary plug-in installed. If they don't, you've got to ask yourself whether they'll find the mere idea of your creation so compelling that they'll put time and effort into finding and downloading the software they need to view it.

Some plug-ins, such as the Flash player from Macromedia, have become so well distributed that you can almost be certain that it'll be installed on most people's computers (check out www. macromedia.com/software/player_census/ for current details). But you can never be too sure. If you're going to be using plug-ins on your pages always make sure that really important content – like contact details, phone numbers, e-mail etc. – can be accessed by everyone, not just the people who can see the plug-in. Do this by including ordinary HTML information.

Adding plug-in media to your page

It's worth saying here that the act of adding plug-in media to your page is the easy bit – all you need to do is point your page in the direction of your file and you're away. The hard bit is learning the programs that will create your file in the first place – but those are the subjects for someone else's book. All you're going to need to know about is the <embed> tag.

The <embed> tag is very similar to the <img> tag except (surprise, surprise) it pulls in multimedia files rather than pictures. It also, unlike the <img> element, requires (for no obvious reason) that you include an end tag (</embed>). You simply specify the dimensions the file will take up in the browser window and the URL that the browser can retrieve the file from. It's also good practice to include information about where the plug-in that can play the file can be located and downloaded. These bits of information are added to the <embed>tag as attributes.

The code you'd need would look like this (here I'm pointing at an imaginary Flash file, hence its .swf suffix):

```
<embed
src="pathToYourPlugIn.swf" (This src attribute points at the
file's URL.)
width=40 height=80 (This sets the dimensions the plug-in
media will take up on the page.)
pluginspage="URLneededToDownLoadPlugIn.htm" (This
attribute – pluginspace – tells your browser where it can download
the plug-in needed to play your file.)
</embed>
```

The attribute pluginspage is included to point the end-user to a page where they can download the plug-in needed to see your creation. The plug-in's publishers should provide details of the pluginspage URL in their documentation.

Different plug-ins are also able to support their own particular attributes, for instance some might have an attribute that would force the plug-in to play as soon as the page is downloaded. Again, what these values should be set to is between you and your plug-in maker's documentation.

131

9

In this chapter you'll learn:

What FTP is
What information you need to get from
your ISP or systems administrator
How to use FTP

Finally getting your site up on the Web is by far the easiest thing we'll have done so far. In fact it only really deserves a chapter of its own because people tend to imagine that it's going to be an incredibly technical exercise. It isn't.

WHAT'S THIS?

FTP

FTP stands for File Transfer Protocol. A protocol is a way for computers to speak to each other and transferring files is what FTP does. That's about it. It's just a way of moving files from one remote computer to another. It's been around almost since the beginning of the Internet and it's what you'll use to publish your site.

The most technical thing you're going to have to do is phone up your service provider or systems administrator – the people who are going to look after the computer on which your site is going to finally live – and ask them for your FTP details. (You might find the information in their documentation or on their Website.) This is the only difficult thing to do as there's absolutely no guessing what they'll tell you.

You need to find out these things:

The *name of your FTP server* – this will be an Internet address which will look something like this:

```
ftp.myServerSpace.co.uk
```

Whether you need a *directory name* or *path name* and what it is.

Your *log in* or *user name*.

Your *password* – your log in and password might (or might not be) the same as the log in and password you use when you use your Internet account.

What the *final Web address* will be – you'll need to know what the final URL of your site will be so you can see it when it's published!

Once you've got this information you'll need to find yourself an FTP client – which is just a high-faluting way of talking about a bit of software that'll do FTP for you. If you're using a WYSIWYG-HTML

133

editor it may have an FTP client built in. If not you'll need to find yourself some other software to do the job – go to www.tucows.com or www.download.com and search for FTP: you'll find there's no shortage of shareware and freeware clients out there.

It doesn't really matter which you choose (unless you choose a truly terrible one – look for how well the FTP software is rated before you download it) – all FTP clients are basically the same. In the example below I've used CuteFTP, an ever-popular client easily available from download sites. Don't worry if what you see isn't exactly the same in the software you choose – either consult the documentation or have a root around in the menus and look for Add or New Connection or something like it. You need to find yourself in a position where the software is asking for the *server name* or *FTP host*, *directory* (maybe), *log in* or *user name*, and *password*.

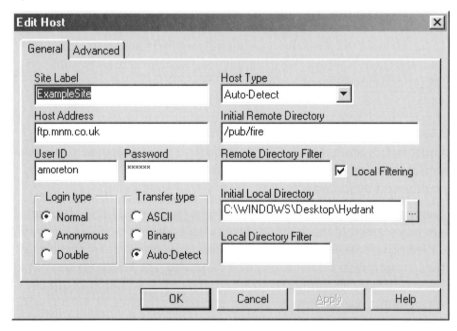

Once you've plugged in your information you'll be presented with a Window's Explorer-like view of your site – except for the fact that the window is broken into two sections. One of these will represent your local site (the site on your computer, the one we're about to publish), the other is your remote site (where you're going to put your files).

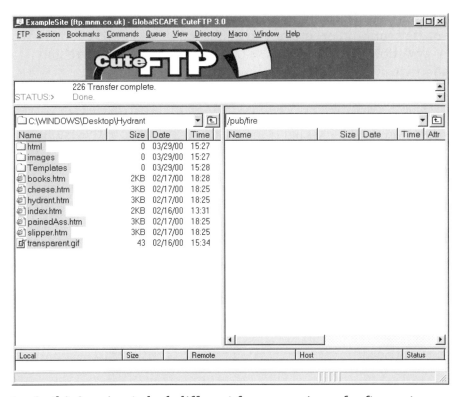

Again this is going to look different from one piece of software to another. However, if your FTP client doesn't show you your two sites – remote and local – side by side you should seriously consider trying another bit of software.

The first time you log on to your FTP server you could find there are already some folders there. In the example above there's a directory called cgi-bin which we certainly didn't create. Don't worry about these unrequested folders – they'll be part of the way your server has been set up by its administrator. The one above would hold CGI scripts (see Chapter 7 if you can't remember about CGI).

Then, and this is the bit that's almost too easy, drag and drop the files from your local site over to your remote site. Your FTP client uploads the files to your site, maybe pausing to dial-up your service provider before it does. When it's done, all the files from your local site should be replicated in the remote site. And there you have it!

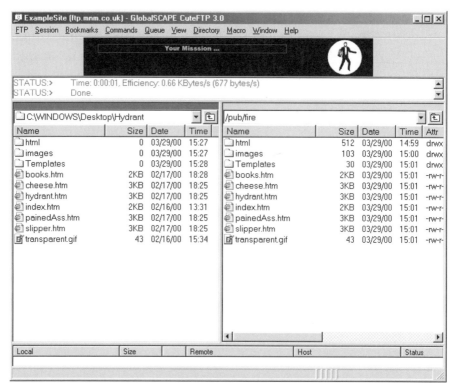

Now you're ready to see if it's all working. Open up your browser and point it at the URL of your site. Assuming nothing's gone terribly wrong you should be proudly admiring your new site – live on the Web!

Of course before you do this you'll have tested your site again and again, making sure links still work and that graphics links aren't broken. You'll have tested in loads of different browsers and nothing will surprise you.

Except it might. Problems that don't reveal themselves when you are testing on your local machine can become terribly apparent when you look at your site over the Web. The most common causes of these problems are simple errors like inconsistent capitalisation in file names (Windows and the Mac don't care how you capitalise; Unix, the main platform for servers, does). But you might find there are problems with download times, in which case you'll need to work out where the bottlenecks are (probably large graphics files) and sort them out. Remember your site will probably be much, much faster on your local machine than it will be over the Web. Once any trouble-shooting's finished with, it's time to try and get some visitors to your site.

In this chapter you'll learn:

About the search sites
About meta tags
How to add keywords
How to add descriptions
About the importance of titles and headings
How to let the search sites know you exist

There are any number of ways for you to publicise your Website – business cards, air writing, shouting, tee-shirts – you know more about your site than anyone and the strategies you dream up to get people to look at it are only limited by your imagination (and budget). However, there are a few bits of HTML that you can add to your pages that'll help people find your site and won't cost you anything. In this chapter we'll be looking at how the to get the search engines and directories to notice you.

Search engines and directories

When people look for stuff on the Web they'll more often than not call up one of the search sites like Alta Vista, Yahoo!, Lycos or whoever and search for whatever it is they're looking for. If they're lucky the site they choose will supply them with a list of URLs all pointing at sites full of the information they were searching for. How do these search sites do it?

Well, they tend to do it in two very different ways. Either by using little pieces of quasi-autonomous software called, amongst other things *spiders*, *robots* and *intelligent agents* or by using real live humans. You'll hear people referring to all search sites as search engines but, strictly speaking, only the sites that use software to create their listings are search engines. Ones that use humans are directories and we'll talk about them first.

The archetypical directory site is Yahoo! (www.yahoo.com) – and they get very sniffy if you go round calling them a search engine. A directory site operates by using teams of human reviewers/librarians whose job it is to check out, précis and classify sites. What's included and where it's included is determined by the site's policies, guidelines, and by human foibles and vagaries. When an end-user searches a directory site they're searching a catalogue organised by humans.

The search-engine driven sites, in contrast, are an almost wholly electronic affair. The search engine sits at the centre of it – an ultra-fast search program capable of simultaneously analysing and returning results to hundreds and thousands of users, taking requests for hundreds and thousands of pages.

The engine looks through its catalogue – an index of hundreds of millions of Web pages all constantly updated by an army of spiders, robots, etc. These scarily named pieces of code are sent out across the Internet looking for Web servers. When they find them they send pages and other information about the site back to the catalogue for *indexing*.

Once a site has been indexed, then it can be found by searching with the search engine. Of course this whole process is transparent to the end-user who couldn't care less how the search engine works as long as they find out what they want to know. But it matters to you because you want them to find your site.

All search sites work in different ways – they want to be the site you use all the time, so they'll try to provide you with the best information and search results they can. That's how they do business and how they sell their advertising. Their job would be a lot easier if there weren't so many, how shall I put this, *disreputable* sites trying to crash on to their listings.

You'll have noticed that the Web is full of people who really want to make sure that you get to know about their particular get-rich-quick scam, dodgy site, or iffy investment scheme. Such people recognise the importance of getting listed in a set of search results (regardless of what you might have searched for) and aren't above trying to manipulate the way the search engine works to get themselves higher listings.

To counter this, the search sites are continually modifying the way their engines operate in the hope of perfecting their search and indexing methods – and of foiling the dodgier sites. Which is all a very long way of telling you that it's very difficult to make hard and fast rules about what's going to get your site indexed: they all work to different rules and those rules are always changing. The advice given here is very general.

Using meta tags

The first thing you need to do to help people find your Website is to add a couple of tags to the <head> element of your pages. These tags are going to add a list of *keywords* – words that a search engine can match to a user's query – and a *description* – the text a search site will display when it returns a list of results. The keywords and descriptions are held in <meta> tags – these are used to tell browsers, search engines and servers information about the document that the end-user doesn't necessarily need to be exposed to. This can be information about copyright, language or authorship, amongst others. When you hear people bandying around the term <meta> tags you can be be pretty sure they're talking about the tags that'll be useful to the search sites.

Adding keywords

When people look for information on a search site they'll tend to do it by entering a word or three into a search field and waiting for their results to come winging their way back to them. You can help people find your page by making a list of the words or phrases you imagine people would use to find your site. So if your site were, for instance, *An Exciting Beginner's Guide To HTML* you might decide that your keywords should be as follows:

```
guide to HTML, HTML, guide, how to make Web
pages, beginners, easy, exciting, make my own Web
pages, Websites, construct, novice, HTML, code,
source, W3C, design, Web design
```

When you're working on your list of keywords try to imagine how somebody else might try to search for a site like yours. How might they phrase their query? It's possible to be too close to your site and its subject to come up with an effective list of keywords so it's worth checking your list with friends, colleagues and family to make sure that the list makes sense to them as well. Once you've created your list you can add it to your code by inserting a <meta> element into the <head> of your page, like so:

```
<head>

<title> An Exciting Beginner's Guide To HTML</ title>

<meta name="keywords" content="guide to HTML,
HTML, guide, how to make Web pages, beginners,
easy, exciting, make my own Web pages, Websites,
construct, novice, HTML, code, source, W3C,
design, Web design">

</head>
```

Because there are loads of different types of <meta> tags, the element
holding our keywords needs to be given two attributes – name and
content. The name is the type of meta tag you're including – in this
case keywords. The content attribute is where you add the value of your
meta tag – this is where you put your actual list of keywords.

Adding a description

You should also add a brief description of your site: what it's about,
who it's for etc. This description can be used by search sites to help
index your pages but its primary use is to provide a quick précis of
your site which can be displayed in a list of search results. A good
succinct description can bring traffic to your site. Descriptions are
added in a very similar way to keywords. Both of them are meta tags,
in fact the only difference is the value of the name attribute, which is
now, unsurprisingly, description. The content attribute will
contain the text that makes up your description.

```
<head>

<title>Description Example</title>

<meta name="description" content="For an
excellent, exciting introduction to the strange
world of HTML visit our site! ">

</head>
```

Of course you can have both a description and a keyword in the
head of the same document. To do this just run one meta after
another as in the example below.

```
<head>

<title>Description Example</title>

<meta name="description" content="For an
excellent, exciting introduction to the strange
world of HTML visit our site! ">

<meta name="keywords" content="guide to HTML,
HTML, guide, how to make Web pages, beginners,
easy, exciting, make my own Web pages, Websites,
construct, novice, HTML, code, source, W3C,
design, Web design">

</head>
```

Titles and headings

Some search sites (mainly older ones) attach a lot of importance to the `<title>` and `<h1>` elements of Web pages – sometimes more than to the keywords and descriptions – so make sure that you give every page a descriptive title and use your h1, h2, h3, etc, elements to structure your documents logically. While it may *look* right to use an `<h1>` to format every big heading in your document, unless those headings really do have most precedence in your document they could confuse a search engine and end up getting you low (or worse) no search-site list placings.

By the same token, if you're planning on using custom CSS styles on your site, remember that search sites may still be looking for `<h1>` tags on your page for indexing purposes. Always wrap important headings and information in structural tags so that search sites will be aware of the importance of your content.

Submitting your site

Despite all this talk of quasi-autonomous software agents and robots and spiders and indexing and descriptions, the Web is now so big that you can't afford to sit back once you've completed your site

143

and wait for it to be indexed – you're going to have to do something to let the search sites know that your site is out there and ready to be visited.

This is a straightforward if repetitive task. Work out a list of the search sites you want to be included on and then visit each of them in turn. Check out their site and, usually, on the first page you'll find a link named 'Submit Your URL' or 'Add Your Site' or something very similar. Each search site follows a slightly different procedure when it comes to submitting your site, but all of them will walk you through what you need to do.

<A>...</A>

attributes: href – name – target – style

This is the link element. Its most common use is to attach an href attribute to it and use it as a link to another URL.

Example `<a href="pathToURL">Click here</a>`

href='*yourChoiceOfURL*'
value: relative or absolute URL

Use the href attribute to point a link to the URL it should be linking to.

Example `<a href="`**`pathToURl.htm`**`"> Click here</a>`

name='*yourChoiceOfName*'
value: any value

Use the name attribute to point at a specific point in a longer document. Then a link element using a href attribute can link directly to that point in the document by using the document's URL followed by a # sign and the value that has been set as a name.

Example `<a name="theMainSection">` Click here to jump to the main section`</a>`

target='nameOfFrameOrWindow'
value: name of frame or
> *_blank*
> *_parent*
> *_self*
> *_top*

The target attribute can either be used within a frameset or to force the creation of a new browser window. To load a link from one frame to another, the frames have to be named in their frameset document. Then the target can be set to the frame's name. If a target is set to a name that isn't in the frameset the link will open in a new window.

There are also four reserved values for the target attribute. _blank creates a new window for the link to open up in. _parent opens the linked document into the frameset containing the frame. This is useful in a nested frameset. _self replaces the current document in the containing frame or window. _top replaces the current document with the linked document.

Example `<a name="yourFileName.htm"` `target="namedFrame">` Click here`</a>`

style='styleSheetProperty'
value: any valid CSS property

The style attribute allows you to set any applicable CSS property using the rules of CSS syntax (for a full guide *see* Appendix 2).

Example `<a style="color:purple">`This is a link in purple`</a>`

<B>...</B>

attributes: style

<b> is a container tag that tells the browser to embolden any text held within it.

Example <b>This will come out bold</b>

style='*styleSheetProperty*'
value: any valid CSS property

The style attribute allows you to set any applicable CSS property using the rules of CSS syntax (for a full guide *see* Appendix 2).

Example <b style="color:blue">This is bold and in blue</b>

<BLOCKQUOTE>...</BLOCKQUOTE>

attributes: style

Blockquote is used to indent text. It was intended to separate long block quotations off from the text that surrounded them. A blockquote is used these days mostly to compensate for HTML's woeful lack of tabs. Note that you can include any number of paragraphs within a blockquote. Also blockquotes can include further blockquotes allowing you to indent within an indent.

Example <blockquote>
          <p> The text to be indented. The first
          paragraph of which goes here.</p>
          <p>The second of which goes here</p>
          </blockquote>

style='*styleSheetProperty*'
value: any valid CSS property

The `style` attribute allows you to set any applicable CSS property using the rules of CSS syntax (for a full guide *see* Appendix 2).

Example `<blockquote style="color:blue; font-`
`style:italic" >`
`<p> The text to be indented. The first`
`paragraph of which goes here.</p>`
`<p>The second of which goes here</p>`
`</blockquote>`

<BODY>...</BODY>
attributes: background – bgcolor – text – link – alink – vlink – style

The body element contains the viewable (or listenable) content in an HTML document. While information *about* the document is contained in its <head>, the <body> contains everything that will be rendered on to the page.

Example `<body>This will render in the body of the`
`document</body>`

background='*pathToYourImageFile.gif*'
value: relative or absolute URL

The background attribute points at an image file that is then tiled behind the main content of the window. Note that there's also a more flexible style attribute, also called background, that achieves the same effect (but you can specify whether it tiles or not).

Example `<body background="pathToYourImageFile.gif">`

bgcolor='*recognizedColorNameOrHexadecimal*'
value: hexadecimal colour value or recognised colour name

Use this attribute to set the background colour of your page. A list of acceptable colour names and their hexadecimal equivalents can be found at http://www.andrewmoreton.co.uk/dreamNotes/colList.htm

Example <body `bgcolor="teal">`

text='*recognizedColorNameOrHexadecimal*'
value: hexadecimal colour value or recognised colour name

The text attribute sets the basic colour of all text displayed in the document.

Example <body `bgcolor="teal"` `text="blue">`

link='*recognizedColorNameOrHexadecimal*'
value: hexadecimal colour value or recognised colour name

The `link` attribute sets the colour that ordinary unvisited text links will display, overriding the usual default colour of blue. A list of acceptable colour names and their hexadecimal equivalents can be found at http://www.andrewmoreton.co.uk/dreamNotes/colList.htm

Example <body `link="red">`

alink='*recognizedColorNameOrHexadecimal*'
value: hexadecimal colour value or recognised colour name

The `alink` (activated link) attribute defines the colour that a text link will change to *while the end user is clicking on it*. A list of acceptable colour names and their hexadecimal equivalents can be found at http://www.andrewmoreton.co.uk/dreamNotes/colList.htm

Example <body `link="red"` `alink="yellow">`

149

vlink='*recognizedColorNameOrHexadecimal*'

value: hexadecimal colour value or recognised colour name

A vlink attribute sets the colour of links that the end-user has already visited. A list of acceptable colour names and their hexadecimal equivalents can be found at http://www.andrewmoreton.co.uk/dreamNotes/colLost.htm

Example <body link="red" alink="yellow"
        vlink="green">

style='*styleSheetProperty*'

value: any valid CSS property

The style attribute allows you to set any applicable CSS property using the rules of CSS syntax (for a full guide *see* Appendix 2). This is the W3C's preferred method for you to set up body tag attributes.

Example <body style="background-color:teal; font-family:Arial; font-style:italic">

Because of the academic roots of HTML the <p> element – which is used to designate paragraphs – tends to put a lot of white vertical space around content that's been marked up as a paragraph. The <br> tag forces text on to the next line without creating a new paragraph and thus avoids the addition of too much white space.

Example <p>use this to force line breaks here
        here <br> and
here</p>

<CITE>...</CITE>

attributes: style

The <cite> element is used to tell the browser that the enclosed content has been taken as reference from another source. Most browsers will tend to display the contents of a cite tag in italics, though CSS styles can be used to control how its content are rendered.

Example `<The above reference was taken from`
`<cite>Physics Made Easy</cite>`

style=*'styleSheetProperty'*
value: any valid CSS property

The `style` attribute allows you to set any applicable CSS property using the rules of CSS syntax (for a full guide *see* Appendix 2).

Example `<cite style="font-family:Arial; font-`
`style:italic">`

<DIV>...</DIV>
attributes: align – id – class – style

The `<div>` element is used to group sections of HTML content within a single tag that can then have a number of attributes set. For example several blocks of running content could all be centred or – using a `style` attribute – positioned on the screen and made to behave like a DTP-style word/picture box (though of course you can mix words and pictures in a single box).

Used in conjunction with CSS-P style attributes, the `<div>` tag gives you the building blocks of HTML page layout.

Example `<div align="center">`
`<h1>A Centered Heading</h1>`
`<p>With some content beneath it.</p>`
`</div>`

align=*'alignment'*
value: left – right – centre

The `align` attribute when used in conjunction with content held in a `<div>` element will align that content in relationship to the placement of the `<div>`.

Example `<div align="center">`
      `<h1>A Centered Heading</h1>`
      `<p>With some content beneath it.</p>`
      `</div>`

id='whatever'

value: anything you like but avoid spaces

Adding an `id` attribute to your `<div>`s can make it easier to identify their content and purpose.

Example `<div id="newsLayer">Here's the News</div>`

class='className'

value: anything you like but avoid spaces

A class attribute tells the browser to format a `<div>` according to instructions from a custom class style. For more information *see* Appendix 2.

Example `<div class=".newsHeadStyle">Here's the`
      `News</div>`

style='styleSheetProperty'

value: any valid CSS property

The `style` attribute allows you to set any applicable CSS property using the rules of CSS syntax (for a full guide *see* Appendix 2). Use this attribute to position and control the dimensions of `<div>` box layout elements.

Example `<div`
      `style='position:absolute;`
      `left:145px;`
      `top:70px;`
      `width:350px;`

```
height:200px;
z-index:1">
  <p>Here's the first para of content</p>
  <p>Here's the second para of content</p>
</div>
```

<EM>...</EM>

attributes: style

Use the <em> tag when you want to emphasise its contents – this is rendered using italics in most browsers; however you can override this using stylesheets.

Example <p>it is **<em>important</em>** that you do is
like this</p>

style='*styleSheetProperty*'

value: any valid CSS property

The `style` attribute allows you to set any applicable CSS property using the rules of CSS syntax (for a full guide *see* Appendix 2).

Example <em **style="font-family:arial; font-
weight:bold">**
Render This!</em>

<FONT>...</FONT>

attributes: colour – face – size – style

The `font` element contains attributes that control the way text held within the element is rendered. The W3C would really prefer it if you didn't use this element and used CSS styles instead.

Example <p>**<font face="Arial, Helvetica, sans-serif"
size="2" color="teal">**Here's the content
</font></p>

153

colour='*recognizedColorNameOrHexadecimal*'
value: hexadecimal colour value or recognised colour name

The `color` attribute changes the colour of the type held within the tag.

Example `<font color="orange">`...`</font>`

face='*nameOfFont*'
value: one of more font names, separated by commas

The `face` attribute gives the browser a list of preferred font faces in which to render an area of text. The first font in the list is taken to be the most favoured font choice and is used if available. If it isn't, the browser will take the second choice, followed by the third and so on. Eventually it will revert to using the browser's default text settings.

The W3C would prefer that you used CSS styles to control which fonts the browsers use to render text.

Example `<font face="Arial, Helvetica, sans-serif">`...`</font>`

size='*number*'
value: number between 1 and 7

The `size` attribute controls the size of type held within a `<font>` tag. Setting a value of 7 will (counter-intuitively) set text to a size slightly bigger than an `<h1>` element, 6 would get you text the same size as an `<h1>`, 5 an `<h2>` and so on right down to 1.

All these values are rendered *in relation to the browser's default font size*. If an end-user has their browser's default set to 48pt then a size value of 3, then size 3 renders as 48 pt. Higher values make the type larger, smaller values make it smaller.

Yet again the W3C would rather you used CSS styles for this. CSS means that you can accurately set the point size of type rather than dealing with unpredictable relative sizes.

Example `<font size="1">...</font>`

style='*styleSheetProperty*'
value: any valid CSS property

The `style` attribute allows you to set any applicable CSS property using the rules of CSS syntax (for a full guide *see* Appendix 2.)

Example `<font style="font-family:arial;`
`font-weight:bold;color:red">`
`Render This!</font>`

<FORM>...</FORM>

attributes: action – method – style

A `<form>` element is used to contain all the `<input>` elements and buttons that make up an HTML form. This is what you use when you need to gather information from your audience. To make use of the data they submit to you, you'll need to have talked to your systems administrator or Internet Service Provider and ask them about using CGI (Common Gateway Interface) to process your form data. For more details *see* Chapter 7 on forms.

Example `<form method="post"`
`action="URLofYourCgiScript.cgi">`
`<p>Your Name Please <input type="text"`
`name="name"></p>`
`<p>Do you eat any of these meals?<br>`
`Breakfast <input type="checkbox"`
`name="meals" value="breakfast">`
`Lunch`
`<input type="checkbox" name="meals"`
`value="lunch">`
`Dinner`
`<input type="checkbox" name="meals"`
`value="dinner">`

155

```
</p>
<p>And are you <br>
 male
 <input type="radio" name="sex"
 value="male">
 female
 <input type="radio" name="sex"
 value="female">
 </p>
 <p>
<input type="submit" name="Submit"
value="Submit">
</p>
</form>
```

action='*URL*'

value: any relative or absolute URL

The action attribute tells the browser where the data in a form is to be submitted. Usually this will point at the URL of a CGI script.

Example `<form method="post"`
        `action="URLofYourCgiScript.cgi">`

method='*method*'

value: get – post

When a browser submits data from a form it needs to have a *method* specified that will control the manner in which the data is submitted. The method that you'll need will be specific to your server and CGI script. Again, talk to your systems administrator or Internet Service Provider for more information.

Example `<form method="post"`
        `action="URLofYourCgiScript.cgi">`

style='*styleSheetProperty*'

value: any valid CSS property

The `style` attribute allows you to set any applicable CSS property using the rules of CSS syntax (for a full guide *see* Appendix 2).

Example `<form method="post"`
`action=" URLofYourCgiScript.cgi"`
`style='color:red; font-family:arial;'>`

<FRAME> ...</FRAME>

attributes: name – frameborder – noresize – scrolling – src

The `<frame>` element is used within a `<frameset>` to set the properties of an individual frame. Some of the properties that you might expect to be set here, particularly the dimensions of the frame, are attributes of the `<frameset>` element.

Example `<frameset rows="50%,50%" cols="50%,50%">`
`<frame src="left.htm" name="left1">`
`<frame src="right.htm" name="right1">`
`<frame src="left.htm" name="left2">`
`<frame src="right.htm" name="right2">`
`</frameset>`

name='*whateverYouLike*'

value: any text – no spaces

Assigning a name attribute to a `<frame>` allows you to target links that are held in another frame. For further explanation of targeting and frames *see* Chapter 6.

Example `<frame src="left.htm" name="left1">`

frameborder='*yes*' or '*no*'
value: yes – no

The frameborder attribute controls whether borders get drawn around individual frames.

Example <frame name="main" src="main.htm"
        frameborder="yes">

noresize

The mere presence of a noresize attribute in a <frame> prevents the end user from resizing a frame. If you don't add a noresize then users can move frames around by dragging at their borders.

Example <frame name="main" src="main.htm" **noresize**>

scrolling='*auto*'or '*no*' or '*yes*'
value: auto – yes – no

Should there be too much content to be displayed in the area allotted a frame then a browser will automatically add scroll bars that will allow access to the hidden content. Setting the scrolling attribute to auto gives the same effect. 'No' will prevent the browser from adding scroll bars, regardless of whether this prevents access to content, and 'yes' will put scroll bars around the frame regardless.

Example <frame name="main" src="main.htm"
        scrolling="yes">

src='*url*'
value: absolute or relative URL

The src attribute is what fills a frame with content. Point it at the URL that you want to populate the frame with.

Example <frame name="main" **src="main.htm">**

<FRAMESET>...</FRAMESET>

attributes: frameborder – rows – cols

The <frameset> element tells a browser to divide up its window into separate sub-windows, each displaying a different URL. The <frameset> element replaces the body in a standard HTML document. The <title> of a frameset is the title that will be rendered in the title bar of the document window. Always included within a <frameset> are two or more <frame> elements, all with their own separate attributes.

Example `<frameset cols="25%,75%" rows="*">`
        `<frame name="nav" src="nav.htm">`
        `<frame name="main" src="main.htm">`
    `</frameset>`

Because framesets operate by dividing up the main browser window into rows and columns to achieve certain effects, you may sometimes need to *nest* one frameset within another. To do this the second frameset needs to be contained within the first.

Example `<frameset cols="25%,75%" rows="*">`
        `<frame name="nav" src="nav.htm">`
        `<frameset cols="75%,25%" rows="*">`
          `<frame name="main" src="main.htm">`
          `<frame name="sidebar"`
          `src"sidebar.htm">`
        `</frameset>`
    `</frameset>`

frameborder='no' or 'yes'
value: no – yes

The frameborder attribute turns on or off borders around *all* frames in the frameset. The borders of individual frames can be turned on or off with a frame-level attribute.

159

Example `<frameset cols="25%,75%" rows="*"`
`frameborder="no">`

rows='*pixels*' or '*percentage*' or '*wildcard*'
value: whole numbers, percentages and *, separated by commas

Use the rows attribute in conjunction with the `<frameset>` element to divide the browser window into – rows! Set the width of the rows with values expressed as pixels, percentages of the browser window or use * – the wildcard value – which will leave the browser to work out how to distribute space to that area.

Example `<frameset rows="80, *" cols="25%,75%" >`

cols='*pixels*' or '*percentage*' or '*wildcard*'
*value: whole numbers, percentages and *, separated by commas*

Use the cols attribute in conjunction with the `<frameset>` element to divide the browser window into – columns! Set the height of the columns with values expressed as pixels, percentages of the browser window or use * – the wildcard value – which will leave the browser to work out how to distribute space to that area.

Example `<frameset rows="80, *" cols="25%,75%">`

<H1>...</H1>, <H2>...</H2>, <H3>...</H3>
<H4>...</H4>, <H5>...</H5>, <H6>...</H6>
attributes: align – style

Use the `<h1>` through to `<h6>` elements to describe the comparative importance of headings within your HTML document. `<h1>` designates the most important heading, `<h6>` the least.

Example `<h1>This the most important heading</h1>`
`<h2>This the second most important`
`heading</h2>`

align=*'alignment'*

value: left – right – centre

Use the alignment attribute to set the alignment of a heading horizontally on a page. You can also set alignment as part of a style attribute – and that's the way the W3C would prefer you did it.

Example <h1 **align="center"**>This is is the most important heading</h1>

style=*'styleSheetProperty'*

value: any valid CSS property

The style attribute allows you to set any applicable CSS property using the rules of CSS syntax (for a full guide *see* Appendix 2).

Example <h1 **style="color:red; font- family:arial;"**>This is the most important heading</h1>

<HEAD>...</HEAD>

The <head> element contains content that isn't displayed directly in the browser window. Usually this means information *about* the document – its title for instance or keywords for search sites. Every HTML document needs to contain a <head>.

Example <html>
    <head>
    <title>This is the title</title>
    </head>
    <body>
        This contains the visible portion of
        the document
    </body>
    </html>

161

<HR>

attributes: align – noshade – size – width – style

Inserting <hr> into your code creates a horizontal rule that can be used to divide up text. Note that an <hr> takes up a whole line of its own so you can't use it between words – it will always create its own paragraph. Also note that the <hr> element doesn't need a closing tag. You can set a variety of attributes for <hr> but the W3C would prefer that you use CSS stylesheets.

Example <hr align="center">

align='*alignment*'

value: left – right – centre

Use the align ment attribute to set the alignment of a horizontal rule.

Example <hr align="center">

noshade

value: n/a

The noshade attribute turns off the default '3D' effect on a horizontal rule.

Example <hr noshade>

size

value: pixels

The size attribute sets the thickness of an hr.

Example <hr size="4">

width
value: pixels or percentage

Use the width attribute to set the width of a horizontal rule. The default width is 100 per cent of the browser window

Example <hr width="50%">

style='*styleSheetProperty*'
value: any valid CSS property

The style attribute allows you to set any applicable CSS property using the rules of CSS syntax (for a full guide *see* Appendix 2).

Example <hr style="color:red">

<HTML>...</HTML>

attributes: n/a

The <html> element is wrapped around every other bit of code in your document. It alerts the browser to the fact that it's going to have to deal with some HTML.

Example <html>
        <head>
        <title>Here's The Title</title>
        </head>

        <body bgcolor="#FFFFFF">
        <h1>A Level 1 Heading </h1>
        <h2>A Level 2 Heading </h2>
        <p>The main bit of the document.</p>
        </body>
        </html>

<I>...</I>

attributes: style

The <i> element is a container that forces the browser to italicise the enclosed text.

Example `<p>The next word will be`
`<i>italicised</i></p>`

style='*styleSheetProperty*'
value: any valid CSS property

The `style` attribute allows you to set any applicable CSS property using the rules of CSS syntax (for a full guide *see* Appendix 2).

Example `<p>The next words will be <i style=`
`"color:red">` italicised and in red`</i></p>`

<IMG>

attributes: align – alt – border – height/width – hspace/vspace –src –style

The `img` element places a graphics files (.gif or .jpeg) into your page. Always add `height` and `width` attributes – this will speed up the browser's rendering of your page.

Example `<img src="pathToYourPicture.gif" height=200`
`width=200>`

align='*where*'
value: bottom – left – middle – right – top

Use the align attributes to control the flow of text around an image (depreciated in HTML 4).

Example `<img src="pathToYourPicture.gif"`
`align="left" height=200 width=200>`

alt='*alternative text message*'
value: anything you write in

Not all browsers support graphics and not all users want to see your pictures. The alt attribute sets a text message that can be rendered instead of a graphic.

Example `<img src="pathToYourPicture.gif" alt="This`
`is a picture" height=200 width=200>`

border='*widthExpressedInPixels*'
value: any number you choose

The border attribute renders a black rectangular border around an image. If the image is doubling up as a link (i.e. it's got an <a> element wrapped around it) the border's colour is set by the document's various link settings. Images acting as links get a 1-pixel border by default – turn this off by setting the border's value to 0. Stylesheets can be used to set a border's colour.

Example `<img src="pathToYourPicture.gif" border=2`
`height=200 width=200>`

height='*heightExpessedInPixels*'
width='*widthExpessedInPixels*'
value: any number you choose

Height and width attributes define the dimensions that a graphics file will take up on a page. You should set these attributes to the exact same size as the image you're including. This will speed up the time your page takes to render. It also allows the browser to hold open space for the image while it downloads, stopping your pages from reflowing as each new picture turns up.

Example `<img src="pathToYourPicture.gif"` **height=200 width=200>**

hspace='horizontalOffsetExpressedInPixels' vspace='verticalOffsetExpressedInPixels'
value: any number you choose

The hspace and vspace attributes set a margin between the image and the other HTML elements that surround it. hspace sets the left and right margins of an image and vspace sets space at the top and bottom.

Example `<img src="pathToYourPicture.gif"` height=200 width=200 **hspace=6 vspace=3>**

src='pathToImageURL'
value: relative or absolute URL

Without the src attribute you'd never get to see your images at all. If no src attribute is set then a broken link marker is rendered in the browser, either at the browser's default size setting or to a size specified by the height and width attributes.

Example `<img` **src="pathToYourPicture.gif"** height=200 width=200>

style='styleSheetProperty'
value: any valid CSS property

The style attribute allows you to set any applicable CSS property using the rules of CSS syntax (for a full guide *see* Appendix 2).

Example `<img src="pathToYourPicture.gif"` height=200 width=200 **style="margin-right: 60px">**

<INPUT>

attributes: type – align – alt – name – src – style

<input> elements add the checkboxes, radio buttons, text fields and so on that make up an HTML form. These bits and pieces are collectively known as *controls*. Set the controls by using the type attribute. Each control can then be assigned further sub-attributes that control the type way data is submitted with the form. Remember you'll always need to wrap your inputs in a <form> tag.

Example <form method="post" action=
         "URLofYourCGI.cgi">
         Your Name Please
         <input type="text" name="name">
         </form>

type='theTypeOfFormControl'
value: checkbox – image – radio – reset – submit – text

type is by far the most important attribute you can assign to an input control: without it nothing would happen. Use type to turn your inputs into checkboxes, radio buttons, text fields, etc. Most (but not all) input controls also require name and value attributes.

Example <input **type="text"** name="name">

The different inputs have their own special sub-attributes as well.

checkbox   Creates checkboxes in a form. Checkboxes can be checked or unchecked and allow an end-user to select several, or no, choices from a group of checkboxes.

The name attribute groups several checkboxes together.

The value attribute is the data that will be sent back to a CGI script when a checkbox has been ticked by an end-users.

The checked attribute ticks a checkbox as a page loads.

167

```
<form method="post" action=
"pointToACgiScript.cgi">
  <p>Are you hungry?</p>
    <p>Very <input type="checkbox"
    name="hungry" value="very">
    Quite <input type="checkbox"
    name="hungry2" value="very">
    Not <input type="checkbox"
    name="hungry2" value="very"
    checked>
  </p>
</form>
```

image   Lets you use a graphic stored at a specified URL as the submit button on a form. Note that you can't set up an image as a reset button.

```
<form method="post" action=
"pointToACgiScript.cgi">
  <input type="image"
  src="pathToMyButtonImage.gif"
  width="50" height="50">
</form>
```

radio   Creates radio buttons in a form. Radio buttons can be clicked on or off but unlike checkboxes only one radio button in a group can be selected.

The name attribute groups several radio buttons together.

The value attribute is the data that will be sent back to a CGI script when a radio button has been ticked by an end-user.

The checked attribute ticks a radio button as a page loads.

```
<form method="post" action=
"pointToACgiScript.cgi">
  <p>What sex are you?</p>
      <p>Male <input type="radio"
      name="gender" value="male">
      Female <input type="radio"
      name="gender" value="female">
  </p>
</form>
```

reset   Creates a button that will flush a form of any entered
             data, letting an end-user start again, change their
             mind or whatever.

             The value lets you set a label that will appear on the
             reset button. If you don't add a value the button
             either says reset or reset form.

```
<form method="post" action=
"pointToACgiScript.cgi">
    <input type="reset" value="Doh!">
</form>
```

submit   Creates a button that will submit data entered in a
             form to the URL specified in the action attribute
             of the <form> element containing the button. This
             is what sends data back to be processed by your
             CGI script.

             The value lets you set a label that will appear on the
             submit button. If you don't add a value the button
             either says submit or submit form.

```
<form method="post" action=
"pointToACgiScript.cgi">
    <input type="submit" value="OK!">
</form>
```

169

text	Creates a text field that allows data entered into it to be submitted with a form's data.
	The `maxlength` sets the maximum number of characters allowed in a field.
	The `size` attribute determines the width of the text field (but it is calculated relative to the size of type surrounding the field, so test carefully).

```
<form method="post" action
="pointToACgiScript.cgi">
        <input type="text" name="name">
    </form>
```

align='*where*'
value: bottom – left – middle – right – top

Should you use an image as a submit button, do this by setting the `type` attribute to `image`. You can then use an `align` attribute to control the flow of text around an image.

Example
```
<input type="image"
    name="myButtonPicture"
    src="pathToMyButtonImage.gif"
    width="50" height="50"
    align="left">
```

alt='*alternative text message*'
value: anything you write in

The `alt` attribute is intended for use with images that will submit a form. (*See* entry above.) Use it to add an alternative text message for end-users without graphical browsers, or for those who view the Web with images turned off.

Example `<input type="image"`
        `name="myButtonPicture"`
        `src="pathToMyButtonImage.gif"`
        `width="50" height="50"`
        `align="left"`
        `alt="This is a picture">`

name=*'aLabelForYourData'*
value: any text you like

To make sense of the data submitted from your form (and in order for a CGI script or other application to process it) you'll have to add a name attribute to every `input` control that directly submits data. In effect this means adding a unique name to every `input` that isn't a `reset` or a `submit` button.

Example `<form method="post" action`
        `="URLofYourCGI.cgi">`
        `Your Name Please <input type="text"`
        `name="name">`
        `</form>`

src=*'pathToImageURL'*
value: relative or absolute URL

If you are using an image as a submit button then use the `src` attribute to tell the browser where that image is.

Example `<input type="image"`
        `src="pathToMyButtonImage.gif">`

style=*'styleSheetProperty'*
value: any valid CSS property

The style attribute allows you to set any applicable CSS property using the rules of CSS syntax (for a full guide *see* Appendix 2).

Example `<input type="text" name="textfield"`
`    style="color:red;">`

<LI>...</LI>

attributes: style

The `<li>` element is used within `<ol>` or `<ul>` (ordered and unordered lists) to separate the different items.

Example `<ul>`
`    <li>Several Items</li>`
`    <li>All In A List</li>`
`    <li>One Item</li>`
`    <li>After Another</li>`
`    </ul>`

style='*styleSheetProperty*'
value: any valid CSS property

The style attribute allows you to set any applicable CSS property using the rules of CSS syntax (for a full guide *see* Appendix 2).

Example `<li style="color:red;">Several Items</li>`

<LINK>

attributes: absolute or relative URL

Against all expectations this element does *not* create hyperlinks. If that's what you're looking for, go over to the `<a>` element now. Use `<link>` instead to let a browser know where to find an external CSS stylesheet. In the future we may be able to use `<link>`s for other purposes, though as yet there's little or no browser support – you've got to use a `rel` attribute (which describes the *relationship* of the `<link>` to the page that contains it). You must put your `<links>` within the `<head>` of your documents.

Example <head>
    <title>Document Title</title>
    <link rel="stylesheet" href=
    "siteStyles.css">
    </head>

<META>

attributes: see below

<meta> tags can contain many different types of information: the sole unifying factor being that the information is intended for the end-user's browser, the server that is distributing the page, or as hooks for search sites.

As no information contained in a <meta> is rendered on to the page it is always held in the <head> of a document. You can use as many as you like.

<meta>s fall into two categories – either they use the http-equiv attribute or they use name. For our purposes the http-equiv attribute is only important for refreshing a document. The name attibute however contains two very important sub-attributes – keyword and description.

Example <html>
    <head>
    <title>Document Title</title>
    <meta http-equiv=3D"refresh"
    content=3D"4;URL=myNextPage.htm">
    </head>
    <body> content in here </body>
    </html>

refresh   Use code like this:

    <meta http-equiv="refresh"
    content="**4**;URL=**myNextPage.htm**">

173

to get a document to stay on screen for a certain amount of time before going to another specified URL. In the example above the emboldened characters (the 4 and the file name) are the variables. The 4 is the number of seconds that the document will stay on screen, the URL is the address of the next document to be seen.

keywords
Keywords let you enter terms you'd like a search engine to match to your page. The words in bold are the variables. Substitute your own set of keywords.

```
<meta name="keywords" content="a list
of keywords, search terms, keywords,
searching, looking for, finding">
```

description
Should your astute choice of keywords match a user's search, then a search site might display the description in its list of potential matches. Some search sites also use a page's description when it comes to indexing a site. Again the emboldened text represents the variable information.

```
<meta name="description" content="For
finding out things about searching this
is the place for you.">
```

<NOFRAMES>...</NOFRAMES>

attributes: n/a

Because not all browsers are able to render framesets it's good practice to put some information within a <noframes> element. A frames-incompatible browser will ignore the frames information and find instead a <body> element contained within the <noframes>.

Example `<noframes>`
```
<body bgcolor="#FFFFFF">
    <p>This page has been designed with
    Frames in mind. Sorry. Here's all
    the information you could possibly
    need.... </p>
</body>
</noframes>
```

<OBJECT>...</OBJECT>

attributes: align – alt – border – height – width – hspace – vspace – src

The `<object>` element is used to add multimedia elements to a Web page – usually ones that require plug-ins to work. It shares every one of its attributes with the `<img>` tag – so look there for further details.

A lot of plug-ins require that you add further proprietary attributes to the `<object>` tag. Check out your documentation for further details.

Example `<object src="generic.obj">`
```
</object>
```

<OL>...</OL>

attributes: style

The `<ol>` element contains the various `<li>` items that make up a list. The o in `<ol>` is for ordered. Ordered lists differentiate themselves from unordered lists by prefacing each list item with a number.

Example `<ol>`
```
    <li>Several Items</li>
    <li>All In A List</li>
    <li>One Item</li>
    <li>After Another</li>
</ol>
```

175

style='*styleSheetProperty*'
value: any valid CSS property

The style attribute allows you to set any applicable CSS property using the rules of CSS syntax (for a full guide *see* Appendix 2).

Example `<ol style="color:red;">>`
```
    <li>Several Items</li>
    <li>All In A List</li>
    <li>One Item</li>
    <li>After Another</li>
</ol>
```

<OPTION>...</OPTION>

attributes: value – style

Used within a `<select>` element which always has to be held in a `<form>` tag, the `<option>` element allows you to define the values displayed on a pop-up list.

Example `<form>`
```
    <select>
        <option value="breakfast">Breakfast
        </option>
        <option value="lunch">Lunch</option>
        <option value="tea">Tea</option>
        <option value="dinner">Dinner
        </option>
        <option value="supper">Supper
        </option>
    </select>
</form>
```

value='anything'
value: any text you like

value sets the information that will be returned to the server from a form where a user selects that particular item.

Example <option **value="supper"**>Supper</option>

style='*styleSheetProperty*'
value: any valid CSS property

The style attribute allows you to set any applicable CSS property using the rules of CSS syntax (for a full guide *see* Appendix 2).

Example <select style="**color:red;**">

<P>...</P>

attributes: align

The <p> element defines the enclosed content as being a paragraph. This means the browser will put space on either side of the element. Use <p> to signal to the browser that, structurally, the enclosed content is a paragraph. Should you simply wish to force a line break use <br>.

Example <p>This contains a paragraph</p>

align='*alignment*'
value: left – right – centre

align is used to control the alignment of a paragraph within either the browser window, or, if contained within a CSS <div> box, the bounds of that box.

Example <p **align="right"**>This contains a paragraph </p>

177

<PRE>...</PRE>

attributes: style

<pre>, meaning preformatted, tells the browser to render the enclosed material in a monospaced typeface. Unlike standard HTML text, which ignores all spaces and returns in the original source HTML, <pre> text honours your linebreaks, spaces, etc.

Example <pre>Make this come out in typewriter
        writing</pre>

style='*styleSheetProperty*'
value: any valid CSS property

The style attribute allows you to set any applicable CSS property using the rules of CSS syntax (for a full guide *see* Appendix 2).

Example <pre **style="color:red;"**>Make this come out
        in typewriter writing</pre>

<SELECT>...</SELECT>

attributes: style

The <select> element is used within a <form> to create a pop-up menu. The <select> element forces the list; held within a <select> must be <option> tags – these contain the items included on the menu.

Example <form>
        <select>
                <option value="breakfast">
                Breakfast</option>
                <option value="lunch">Lunch</option>
                <option value="tea">Tea</option>
                <option value="dinner">Dinner</option>
                <option value="supper">Supper</option>
        </select>
        </form>

style='*styleSheetProperty*'
value: any valid CSS property

The style attribute allows you to set any applicable CSS property using the rules of CSS syntax (for a full guide *see* Appendix 2).

Example `<select style="color:red;">`

<SPAN> ...</SPAN>

attributes: style

Use `<span>` when you want to apply CSS rules to small areas of HTML content. For instance you may have a `<p>` element with a style rule controlling it but want the browser to render some of that `<p>` in a bolder style. A `<span>` acts as a container to which you can assign style rules that override the `<p>`'s settings.

Example
```
<p style="color:teal; font-family:arial;">
     It's important that you #
     <span style="color:blue; font-family:impact;>
     notice this notice
     </span>
     </p>
```

style='*styleSheetProperty*'
value: any valid CSS property

The style attribute allows you to set any applicable CSS property using the rules of CSS syntax (for a full guide *see* Appendix 2).

Example
```
<span style="color:blue; font-family:impact;>
     notice this notice</span>
```

179

<STRONG>...</STRONG>

attributes: style

The strong tag tells the browser that the content held in it needs to be emphasised strongly. It's up to the browser how it does this. Most graphical browsers will render content in bold.

Example `<p>I'd like you to be <strong>very</strong> careful</p>`

style='*styleSheetProperty*'
value: any valid CSS property

The style attribute allows you to set any applicable CSS property using the rules of CSS syntax (for a full guide *see* Appendix 2).

Example `<strong style="color:blue; font-family: impact;> Take note</strong>`

<STYLE>...</STYLE>

attributes: n/a

The `<style>` element always lives in the `<head>` of a document and is used to hold the style rules that will control how a stylesheet-compatible browser renders various elements. The `<style>` element, as yet, only carries one significant attribute, type. This lets the browser know that you're using CSS as opposed to any other (yet to be invented) stylesheet mechanism. Remember to wrap your styles in `<!--` and `-->` to stop older browser from seeing this code.

Example <head>
        <title>Some Styles</title>
        <style type="text/css">
            <!--
            body { font-family: Arial, Helvetica,
            sans-serif; font-size: 24px; line-
            height: 30px}
            h1 { font-size: 36px; color: navy}
            -->
        </style>
        </head>

<TABLE>...</TABLE>

attributes: align – background – bgcolor – border – bordercolour – cellpadding – cellspacing – height – width

The <table> element allows you to use HTML to control the way a browser displays tabular data. Although people have been using tables to control page layout for years, the practice is not encouraged by the W3C, who would prefer you to use <div> boxes and styles to position your content. The <table> element tells the browser that a table is on its way. The actual contents of the cells are defined within the <table> element using <tr> and <td>.

Example **<table>**
        <tr>
        <td>Cell 1</td>
        <td>Cell 2</td>
        </tr>
        <tr>
        <td>Cell 3</td>
        <td>Cell 4</td>
        </tr>
        </table>

align='*where*'
value: bottom – left – middle – right – top

Use the align attributes to control the flow of text around a table.

Example `<table align="left">`

background='*pathToYourImageFile.gif*'
value: relative or absolute URL

The `background` attribute points at an image file that is then tiled behind your table.

Example `<table background="pathToYourImageFile.gif">`

bgcolor='*recognizedColorNameOrHexadecimal*'
value: hexadecimal colour value or recognised colour name

Use this attribute to set the background colour of a table. A list of acceptable colour names and their hexadecimal equivalents can be found in Appendix 3.

Example `<table bgcolor="teal">`

border='*widthExpressedInPixels*'
value: any number you choose

The `border` attribute renders a black rectangular border around a table and every cell in it. Use the `bordercolor` attribute to control the colour of those borders.

Example `<table border=2>`

bordercolor=*'recognizedColorNameOrHexadecimal'*
value: hexadecimal colour value or recognised colour name

Use the bordercolour attribute to control the colour of borders in a table.

Example <table `bordercolor="navy">`

cellpadding=*'pixels or percentage'*
value: pixels – percentage

The `cellpadding` attribute adds clear, empty space between the inside borders of each cell and its content.

Example <table border="1" `cellpadding="5">`

cellspacing=*'pixels or percentage'*
value: pixels – percentage

The `cellspacing` attribute adds clear, empty space between the outside borders of each cell.

Example <table border="1" `cellspacing="5">`

height=*'pixels or percentage'*
value: pixels – percentage

The height attribute defines the height of a table, either in pixels or as a percentage of the browser window.

Example <table `height="400">`

width=*'pixels or percentage'*
value: pixels – percentage

The width attribute defines the width of a table, either in pixels or as a percentage of the browser window.

Example <table `width="400">`

<TD>...</TD>

attributes: align – bgcolor – colspan – height – width – rowspan – style – valign

<td> is the container for any content you want to be held in a specific `table` cell. It has a whole slew of attributes that control various aspects of the cell and the way that content is rendered in it.

Example
```
<table>
  <tr>
    <td>Some Cell Content</td>
    <td>More Cell Content</td>
  </tr>
</table>
```

align='*where*'
value: left – centre – right

Use `align` to align content horizontally in a <td>.

Example <td **align="right"**>some content</td>

bgcolor='*recognizedColorNameOrHexadecimal*'
value: hexadecimal colour value or recognised colour name

Use this attribute to set the background colour of a table cell. A list of acceptable colour names and their hexadecimal equivalents can be found at http://www.andrewmoreton.co.uk/dreamNotes/colList.htm

Example <td **bgcolor="teal"**>some content</td>

colspan='*positiveNumberAbove1*'
value: positive whole number above 1

Use colspan to merge cells together across table columns. The value you give it is equal to the number of columns you want the <td> to take up in a table.

Example <table>
      <tr>
        <td **colspan**="3">This cell takes up
three columns</td>
     </tr>
     <tr>
       <td>1</td>
       <td>2</td>
       <td>3</td>
     </tr>
    </table>

height=*'pixels or percentage'*
value: pixels – percentage

The height attribute defines the height of a <td>, either in pixels or as a percentage of the browser window.

Example <td **height**="400">

width=*'pixels or percentage'*
value: pixels – percentage

The width attribute defines the width of a <td>, either in pixels or as a percentage of the browser window.

Example <td **width**="400">

rowspan=*'positiveNumberAbove1'*
value: positive whole number above 1

Use rowspan to merge cells together across rows. The value you give it is equal to the number of rows you want the <td> to take up in a table.

Example ```<table>
        <tr>
        <td>1</td>
        <td rowspan="3">This cell takes up all
        three of this table's three
            rows </td>
          <td>1</td>
        </tr>
        <tr>
            <td>2</td>
            <td>2</td>
        </tr>
        <tr>
            <td>3</td>
            <td>3</td>
        </tr>
    </table>```

style='*styleSheetProperty*'
value: any valid CSS property

The `style` attribute allows you to set any applicable CSS property using the rules of CSS syntax (for a full guide *see* Appendix 2).

Example ```<td style="color:blue; font-family:impact;>
        Take note</td>```

valign='*where*'
value: top – bottom – middle – baseline

Use `valign` to control the vertical alignment of content held in a `<td>`.

Example ```<td valgin="top">The content of this cell is
        rendered at the top<td>```

<TEXTAREA>...</TEXTAREA>

attributes: cols – name – rows

Very similar to the form-input control text, <textarea> creates a rectangular area into which the end-user can enter data. Unlike text, a <textarea> can contain multiple lines. <textarea>s are usually used as part of a <form>. Because the tag is a container you can add content that is added to the text area as the page is loaded. If the content exceeds the height of the <textarea> the browser will add scroll bars to it.

Example <textarea name="details">Please fill in with details</textarea>

cols='*widthInCharacters*'

value: any number

Use cols to set the number of characters that will fill the width of a <textarea>. The width the browser sets tends to be based on the browser's internal, preference settings, particularly the monospaced font.

Example <textarea **cols="40"** name="details">Please fill in with details</textarea>

name='*uniqueIdentifier*'

value: any text you like

Use the name attribute with a <textarea> to uniquely identify data being submitted from a <textarea> held in a <form>.

Example <textarea **name="details"**>Please fill in with details</textarea>

rows='heightInCharacters'
value: any number

Use rows to set the number of rows of text visible within a
<textarea>. If this means that there's more text than is visible in
the <textarea> the browser will automatically add scroll bars.

Example <textarea **rows="3"**>Please fill in with
        details</textarea>

<TITLE>...</TITLE>

attributes: n/a

The <title> element always lives in the <head> of a page. The
<title> is rendered by browsers into the title bar of a browser
window and is used to label Favourites or Bookmarks set by users.

Example <head><title>The Name of the Page</title>
        </head>

<TR>...<TR>

attributes: align – bgcolor – style – valign

The <tr> element is used within <table>s to hold rows of <td>s.
The <td>s represent the actual cells containing data. Any individual
<td>'s attributes will override attributes applied to the <tr>. Each
successive <tr> creates a new row of cells in a table.

Example <table>
        <tr><td>row 1 cell 1</td>
            <td>row 1 cell 2</td>
        </tr>
        <tr><td>row 2 cell 1</td>
            <td>row 2 cell 2</td>
        </tr>
        </table>

align='*where*'
value: left – centre – right

Use align to align content horizontally in a <tr>.

Example <tr align="right">

bgcolor='*recognizedColorNameOrHexadecimal*'
value: hexadecimal colour value or recognised colour name

Use this attribute to set the background colour of a row of table cells. A list of acceptable colour names and their hexadecimal equivalents can be found in Appendix 3.

Example <tr bgcolor="teal">

style='*styleSheetProperty*'
value: any valid CSS property

The style attribute allows you to set any applicable CSS property using the rules of CSS syntax (for a full guide *see* Appendix 2).

Example <tr style="color:blue; font-family:Impact;>

valign='*where*'
value: top – bottom – middle – baseline

Use valign to control the vertical alignment of content held in a <tr>.

Example <tr valgin="top">

<U>...</U>

attributes: style

Text content wrapped in the <u> element is underlined when rendered.

Example <u>underline this</u>

style='*styleSheetProperty*'
value: any valid CSS property

The style attribute allows you to set any applicable CSS property using the rules of CSS syntax (for a full guide *see* Appendix 2).

Example <tr style="color:blue; font-family: Impact;>

<UL>...</UL>

attributes: type – style

The <ul> element contains the various <li> items that make up a list. The u in <ul> is for unordered. Unordered lists differentiate themselves from ordered lists by prefacing each list item with a bullet point rather than a number.

Example <ul>
            <li>Several Items</li>
            <li>All In A List</li>
            <li>One Item</li>
            <li>After Another</li>
        </ul>

type='*kind of bullet*'
value: circle – disc – square

You can control the type of bullet rendered in <ul>s by setting a type attribute. Use circle, disc or square as values.

Example `<ul type="square">`
`        <li>Several Items</li>`
`        <li>All In A List</li>`
`        <li>One Item</li>`
`        <li>After Another</li>`
`    </ul>`

style=*'styleSheetProperty'*
value: any valid CSS property

The `style` attribute allows you to set any applicable CSS property using the rules of CSS syntax (for a full guide *see* Appendix 2).

Example `<ul style="color:red;">>`
`        <li>Several Items</li>`
`        <li>All In A List</li>`
`        <li>One Item</li>`
`        <li>After Another</li>`
`    </ul>`

191

While I'm sure that you've read and digested the earlier chapters in this book, which discussed using CSS for layout and formatting purposes, it's worth reiterating a few things.

- CSS only works with 4+ versions of the big browsers
  - and even then implementation can be dodgy;
  - Netscape 4.* is very idiosyncratic, though later versions are better;
  - test and test and test again.
- You can use CSS to control formatting both inline and out-of-line by:
  - linking to external CSS files;
  - placing CSS information in the <head> of a document;
  - using it to control a block level element;
  - using it to control inline content with a <span> tag.

CSS and inheritance

Within CSS lurks the concept of *inheritance*. Inheritance allows certain style characteristics to be passed from one element to another. It means that if you tell a <body> tag to use the font Verdana (<body style="font-family: Verdana;">) then every text item held within the body will be rendered in Verdana.

Any <h1> or <p> element held within that <body> tag would *inherit* this style setting as well. Whatever the browser's default settings for <h1>s and <p>s, every piece of text should (unless told otherwise) inherit the <body> tag's text formatting.

In the diagram below you can see how inheritance passes itself through the various levels of a <body> tag. Any inheritable formatting applied to the <body> would apply to *all* the elements held within the <body> tag. However if you wanted to override that formatting you could tell the <div>s in the document that they were formatted differently – then the <p>s, <span>s and <a>s held within the <div>s would inherit that different format.

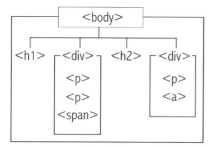

The example below sets the body text to Verdana (which then becomes the default font for the page) and the <h2> to Arial (which overrides our defaults for this particular <h2>).

```
<body style="font-family:Verdana;">
<h1>Welcome To My World</h1>
<h2 style="font-family:Arial;">It's a crazy,
crazy world</h2>
<p>And I'm a crazy kind of guy etc etc etc</p>
<p>Ain't it the truth etc etc</p>
</body>
```

Block-level elements

Also important to CSS is the idea of *block*-level elements. These are elements such as <p> and <h1> that define HTML content so that, when rendered, they force the browser to create a new line of content, or, in the case of the <div> and <span> elements, can be deemed to have a rectangular *block* surrounding them.

193

A block is comprised of *content*, *border*, *margin*, and *padding*. At the centre of this block is the *content*. This is surrounded by clear space which acts as a buffer or *padding* between the contents and the *border* of the block. Finally there can be more clear space between the border and other nearby block elements and these are the *margins*. The dimensions of the whole block are determined by measuring the final lengths of the margins.

You can control all these attributes with CSS. Until you set a specific attribute to control these values they are all initially set to zero and so have no effect. If the size of content in a block is greater than the space allowed it, the default behaviour of a browser will respect any width values set, but expand downwards to display potentially hidden content. You are given some control of this behaviour via the overflow element.

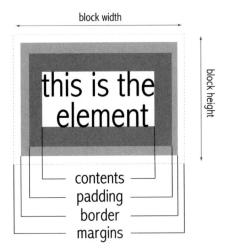

Syntax

CSS syntax is based around property : value pairs which are separated by semi-colons. For a full explanation, reread Chapter 3. If you're using out-of-line styles (holding CSS in the <head> of a document or in an external stylesheet) then your styles information will look like this:

```
selector  {property1:value;
               property2:value;
          }
```

or, with real attributes filled in:

```
h1          {font-family:"Arial;
               background-color:red;
          }
```

Inline styles are added like so:

```
<element style="property1:value; property2:
value;">content goes here</element>
```

or with real attributes:

```
<h1 style="font-family:Arial; background-
color:red;">Here's the content</h1>
```

Shorthand

A good number of CSS attributes are very repetitive in their naming and even more repetitious to code. There are at least five font-based attributes for instance. CSS allows me to write it as below, with lots of redundant repetition of the word font:

```
h3     {font-family: Arial; font-size: 18px; font-
weight: bold; }
```

To alleviate the tedium of this boring work CSS provides a number of *shorthand* properties for the grouping of related attributes. So, instead of the above, you can write

```
h3 {  font: bold 18px Arial }
```

URLs

If you need to use CSS to point at a specific URL (as a background image for instance) you need to specify it using a different syntax from HTML, which looks like this:

```
property: url(thePathToMyFile.html)
```

195

Notice that the URL is held in brackets. Here is an example using proper code:

```
<h2 background-image: url(myImage.gif)>Some
content goes here</h2>
```

Units of measurement

HTML was never designed for page layout and never really developed any accurate ways of measuring anything. CSS, however, allows you to measure things according to the several different systems, as listed below.

Do note that support for these measurements is handled differently in each browser. Pixels are usually the safest bet.

cm – centimetres
em – ems (this is a typographic unit traditionally based on the size of a lower-case m in a given font); browser implementation may vary;
ex – exes (another typographical unit, this time based on the size of a lower-case x)
in – inches
mm – mm
pi – picas
pt – points
px – pixels

CSS attributes

background

inherited: no
use with: all elements
value: any or all of the background styles separated by a space

Use background as shorthand to set a group of background attributes in one statement.

Out-of-line example
```
h1 { background: url(myImage.gif) no-repeat scroll 50% 50%}
```

Inline example
```
<body style="background: url(myImage.gif) no-repeat 50%"}>
```

background-attachment

inherited: no
use with: any element using a background image
value: fixed – scroll

Used in conjunction with the other background attributes, background-attachment allows you to set how a background image moves as an element moves in the browser window. A fixed value stays in place as the rest of an element's content is scrolled up or down. A scroll value will move the image up and down with the element's content.

Out-of-line example
```
body {
background-attachment: fixed;
background-image: url(myImage.gif);
background-position: 200px 100px}
```

Inline example
```
<div style="background-attachment: scroll;
            background-image: url(myImage.gif);>
```

197

background-image

inherited: no
use with: any element
value: any absolute or relative-image URL surrounded by brackets ( )

Use `background-image` to point to a URL which will then be placed behind the content of an element. If you don't specify a `background-attachment` attribute your image will tile as many times as it needs to behind the element.

Out-of-line example
`body {background-image: url(pathToMyImage)}`

Inline example
`<H1 style="background-image: url(pathToMyImage);">`
`Here's the content</H1>`

background-color

inherited: no
use with: any element
value: hexadecimal colour value or recognised colour name

Use `background-color` to set a background colour for an element. Its default state is transparent.

Out-of-line example
`body {background-color: steelblue}`

Inline example
`<div style="background-color: steelblue;">Here's`
`the content</div>`

background-position

inherited: no
use with: any element using background images
value: percentage (%) (*%) – length (x y) – top – centre – bottom – left – centre – right*

Use background-position in conjunction with background-image to place the image precisely in the background of the selected element.

Positioning by percentage is measured as a percentage of an element's surrounding block, the first of which defines the horizontal position, the second the vertical. Any two values need separating with a space.

Positioning by length allows you to use any CSS-acceptable measurements, again the first coordinate defines the horizontal position, the second the vertical. It's also possible to mix length and percentage positioning.

Finally there are the sets of values intended to be used in pairs, such as top right, top left, or bottom center

Out-of-line example
```
body {background-image: url(myImg.gif);
     background-repeat: no-repeat}
     background-position: 50% 50%; }
```

Inline example
```
<div style="background-image: url(myImage.gif);
            background-repeat: no-repeat}
            background-position: 200px 100px;}>
```

background-repeat
inherited: no
use with: any element with a background image
value: no-repeat – repeat – repeat-x – repeat-y

Use background-repeat with background-image to control how often a background-image repeats behind an element. No-repeat renders the image just the once; where the image renders can be controlled using background-position. Use repeat-x and repeat-y to tile the image on a single axis. Repeat is the same as the default behaviour associated with using a background-image – the image tiles throughout the whole of the affected element.

199

Out-of-line example
```
body {background-image: url(myImg.gif);
      background-repeat: no-repeat}
      background-position: 50% 50%;  }
```

Inline example
```
<div style="background-image: url(myImage.gif);
            background-repeat: no-repeat}
            background-position: 200px 100px;}>
```

border
inherited: no
use with: all elements
value: acceptable border – border-width – border-style – colour values

border sets attributes for each border surrounding an element. Use border to set a group of border attributes in one statement.

Out-of-line example
```
h2 {border: double 5px red;}
```

Inline example
```
<p style="border: double 5px red">
```

border-bottom
border-right
border-left
border-top
inherited: no
use with: all elements
value: acceptable border – border-width – border-style –colour values

border-bottom, border-right, border-left and border-top set attributes for the individual borders surrounding an element. Use them to set groups of border attributes in more manageable statements.

Out-of-line example
```
h2 { border-bottom: groove 4px navy; border-top:
ridge 2px green}
```

Inline example
```
<p style="border-bottom: groove 4px navy; border-
top: ridge 2px green;">And here's the content</p>
```

border-bottom-color
border-right-color
border-left-color
border-top-color
inherited: no
use with: all elements
value: hexadecimal colour value or recognised colour name

`border-bottom-color`, `border-right-color`, `border-left-color` and `border-top-color` set the colours of the individual borders surrounding an element. Use these with extreme caution as browser implementation is negligible or buggy.

Out-of-line example
```
.colourfullBorders {border-bottom-color: teal;
                    border-left-color: blue;
                    border-top-color: steelblue;
                    border-right-color: purple;
                    border-width: 4px;
                    }
```

Inline example
```
<h1 style="border-width-top:4px;
           border-bottom-color:teal;
           border-left-color:blue;
           border-top-color:steelblue;
           border-right-color:purple;>
           Here's some content</h1>
```

201

border-bottom-style
border-right-style
border-left-style
border-top-style
inherited: no
use with: all elements
value: dashed – dotted – double – groove – hidden – inset – none – outset – ridge – solid

`border-bottom-style`, `border-right-style`, `border-left-style` and `border-top-style` set the styles that individual borders surrounding an element will render with. Browser support for these styles is patchy so remember to test.

Out-of-line example
```
.allStyles    {border-bottom-style: dashed;
                border-left- style: dotted;
                border-top- style: ridge;
                border-right- style: solid;
                border-with: 4px;
                }
```

Inline example
```
<h1 style="border-width-top:4px;
            border-bottom-style:double;
            border-left-style:dotted;
            border-top-style:ridge;
            border-right-style:groove;>
            Here's some content</h1>
```

border-bottom-width
border-right-width
border-left-width
border-top-width
inherited: no
use with: all elements
value: any CSS length value

`border-bottom-width`, `border-right-width`, `border-left-width` and `border-top-width` set the widths of the individual borders surrounding an element. Browser support for these styles is patchy so remember to test.

Out-of-line example
```
.allStyles   {border-bottom-width: 3px;
              border-left-width: 8px;
              border-top-width: 4px;
              border-right-width: 2px;
              }
```

Inline example
```
<h1 style=" border-bottom-width:4px;
            border-left-width:6px;
            border-top-width:3px;
            border-right-width:2px;>
            Here's some content</h1>
```

border-color
inherited: no
use with: all elements
value: hexadecimal colour value or recognised colour name

`border-color` sets the colour of all the individual borders surrounding an element. Browser implementation is buggy and unpredictable.

Out-of-line example
```
.colourfullBorders {border-color: teal; border-
width:4px}
```

Inline example
```
<h2 style="border-color: teal; border-width:4px">
stuff</h2>
```

border-style

inherited: no
use with: all elements
value: dashed – dotted – double – groove – hidden – inset – none –
outset – ridge – solid

`border-style` sets the style of all the borders surrounding an element. Yet again, browser implementation is buggy and unpredictable.

Out-of-line example
`.colourfullBorders {border-style: groove; border-width:4px}`

Inline example
`<h2 style="border-style: ridge; border-width:4px">stuff</h2>`

border-width

inherited: no
use with: all elements
value: any CSS length value

`border-width` sets the widths of all borders surrounding an element. Yet again, browser implementation is buggy and unpredictable.

Out-of-line example
`.colourfullBorders {border-width:4px}`

Inline example

`<h2 style="border-width:4px">stuff</h2>`

clear

inherited: no
use with: any element
value: both – left – none – right

Use the clear attribute when you have an element using a float attribute and you want to make sure that subsequent content is displayed on a separate line from the floating element.

Out-of-line example
```
.customStyle {clear:right}
```

Inline example
```
<img src="yourImage.gif style="float:right;">
<p style="clear:left;">content</p>
```

color
inherited: yes
use with any element
value: hexadecimal colour value or recognised colour name

Use color to set the colour of text in an element.

Out-of-line example
```
h2 {color:steelblue}
```

Inline example
```
<h2 style="color:steelblue;">Here's the content
</h2>
```

float
inherited: no
use with: any element
value: left – right – none

Use float to take an element out of the normal flow of a page and have other elements flow around it. This attribute is analogous to the now depreciated HTML attribute align.

Out-of-line example
```
.pictureBox {float:left}
```

Inline example
`<IMG src="pathtoYourImage.gif style="float:left;">`

font
inherited: yes
use with: any elements
value: any or all of the background styles separated by a space

Use font as shorthand to set a group of font attributes in one statement.

Out-of-line example
`.priceStyle {font: bold 18pt}`

Inline example
`<p style="font:bold 18pt;">Here's the content</p>`

font-family
inherited: yes
use with: any elements
value: named fonts, separated by spaces

The font-family attribute is used to set a list of possible fonts to be used when rendering an element. The first font on the list is the choice of preference, subsequent fonts are used if the font of preference isn't installed on an end-user's system. If the name of the font you want to use contains more than one word, wrap the name in quotes.

Out-of-line example
`h2 {font-family: Arial, Helvetica, Verdana}`

Inline example
`<h2 style="font-family: "ultra cool", Helvetica, Verdana">Here's the content</h2>`

font-size
inherited: yes
use with: any elements
value: any CSS length value

Use font-size to set the size of type.

Out-of-line example
```
.bodyCopy {font-size:14px}
```

Inline example
```
<p style="font-family:Arial, Helvetica; font-size:18px">Here's the content</p>
```

font-style
inherited: yes
use with: any elements
value: normal – italic

Use font-style to set fonts to italic or normal.

Out-of-line example
```
.italicText {font-style:italic;}
```

Inline example
```
<p style="font-style:italic">Here's the content</p>
```

font-weight
inherited: yes
use with: any elements
value: bold – bolder – lighter – normal

Use font-weight to instruct the browser to embolden or lighten a font.

Out-of-line example
```
.vBoldText {font-weight:bolder;}
```

207

```
<p style="font-weight:bolder;">Here's the
content</p>
```

height
inherited: no
use with: positionable <div> boxes and other block-level elements
value: any CSS length value

The height attribute is used to control the height of <div> boxes and other block-level elements. Note that many browsers will expand an element to a size larger than that specified by height if the content held in the box is bigger than the space it has been allocated.

Out-of-line example
```
.leadStory {height:300px; background-color:
steelblue;}
```

Inline example
```
<div style="height:300px; background-color:
steelblue;>Here's the content</div>
```

letter-spacing
inherited: yes
use with: any text element
value: any CSS length value

Use letter-spacing to add horizontal space or *kerning* between characters.

Out-of-line example
```
.spacedOut {letter-spacing:4em;}
```

Inline example
```
<p style="letter-spacing:5px;">Here's the
content</p>
```

line-height
inherited: yes
use with: any text element
value: any CSS length value

Use `letter-spacing` to add horizontal space or *leading* between lines of text. Browser support for this attribute is buggy and idiosyncratic, so test widely.

Out-of-line example
`.lotsOfLeading {line-height:3px;}`

Inline example
`<p style="line-height:3px;">Here's the content</p>`

margin
inherited: no
use with all elements
value: any CSS length value

Use `margin` as shorthand to set the thickness of all the margins surrounding an element in one statement. You can use a single value to set all margins to the same thickness, or four consecutive values to set the top, right, bottom and left margin width.

Out-of-line example
`h1 {margin:10px 15px 10px 5px}`

Inline example
`<div style="margin:10px 15px 10px 5px;">`

overflow
inherited: no
use with: any <div> box
value: visible – hidden – scroll

The overflow attribute determines how a browser should behave when the content included in a <div> box is bigger than the dimensions allotted it using width and height. The default setting for most browsers is visible, which means the <div> will expand to display the content included. However, a value of hidden will mask extra content and scroll will add a scroll bar, allowing users to navigate up and down the hidden content.

None of this will work unless the <div> has a position:absolute attribute attached to it.

Out-of-line example
```
.scrollBox {: "auto"}
```

Inline example
```
<div style="position:absolute; left:20px; top:20px; width:100px; height:155px; overflow:scroll; ">Here's some stuff.</div>
```

padding
inherited: no
use with: all elements
value: any CSS length value

padding sets attributes for the space in between the content of an image and the border of the block containing it. You can use a single value to set all padding to the same thickness, or four consecutive values to set the top, right, bottom and left padding width.

Out-of-line example
```
h2 {padding:5px}
```

Inline example
```
<p style="padding:5px 3px 8px 2px">content</p>
```

padding-bottom
padding-right
padding-left
padding-top
inherited: no
use with: all elements
value: any CSS length value

Use `padding-bottom`, `padding-right`, `padding-left` and `padding-top` to set attributes for the individual padding buffering an element.

Out-of-line example
```
h2 { padding-bottom: 10px}
```

Inline example
```
<div style="padding-bottom:5px;">And here's the content</p>
```

position
inherited: no
use with: <div> boxes and other block-level elements
value: absolute – relative

Use `position` to place `<div>` boxes and other block-level items in the browser window. A value of `absolute` will let you precisely position content using co-ordinates derived from the top and left corner of the browser window. Relative positioning is not well supported in older browsers, but allows you to position content relative to current dimensions of a browser window.

Out-of-line example
```
.box {position:absolute; top:20px; left:20px;}
```

Inline example
```
<div style="position:relative; top:12%; left:50%;">
Here's the content</div>
```

text-align

inherited: yes
use with: text in any element
value: centre – left – right – justify

Use `text-align` to control the alignment of text within an element. `Center`, `left` and `right` all enjoy widespread browser support but `justify` may confront you with strange results.

Out-of-line example
`.blockText {text-align:justify;}`

Inline example
`<div style="text-align:justify;">Here's the content</div>`

text-decoration

inherited: yes
use with: text in any element
value: line-through – underline – none

Use `text-decoration` to add `underline` and `line-through` styles to your text. You can also use a none value to remove the default underlines from text-based hyperlinks.

Out-of-line example
`.important {text-decoration:underline;}`

Inline example
`<a href="pathToURL" style="text-decoration:none;}>`
`Here's the content</a>`

text-indent

inherited: yes
use with: text in any element
value: any CSS length value

Use text-indent to set the indent of the *first line* of text in an element.

Out-of-line example
```
.firstLineIndent {text-indent:4px;}
```

Inline example
```
<div style="text-indent:4px;">Here's the
content</div>
```

width

inherited: no
use with: positionable <div> boxes and other block-level elements
value: any CSS length value

The width attribute is used to control the width of <div> boxes and other block-level elements. Note that many browsers will expand an element to a size larger than that specified by width if the content held in the box is bigger than the space it has been allocated.

Out-of-line example
```
.leadStory {width:150px; background-color:
steelblue;}
```

Inline example
```
<div style="width:150px; background-color:
steelblue;>Here's the content</div>
```

z-index

inherited: no
use with: positionable <div> boxes and other block-level elements
value: any whole number

The z-index attribute controls the stacking order of positional <div> boxes and other block-level elements. The lower the value given to an element, the further it is towards the bottom of the stacking order. For further information *see* Chapter 4.

Out-of-line example
`.bottomBlock {z-index:1}`

Inline example
`<div style="z-index:3;">`Here's the content`</div>`

A

Absolute pathnames 33
'action' attribute 156
Alignment 151, 161–2, 164, 170, 177, 182, 184, 189, 212
'alink' attribute 149
'alt' attribute 94, 165, 170
Alta Vista 139
Anchor (<a>) element 40
ASCII 6
Attributes 36
Audience for a site 29

B

Background attributes 148, 182, 196–9
Bandwidth 32

BBEdit 2
Beatnik Player 130
Berners-Lee, Tim 5–7, 16–17
'bgcolor' attribute 149, 182, 184, 189
Block level elements 193–4
<blockquote> element 23–5, 147
<body> element 19, 148
Bold text 22, 147
Bookmarks 115
Border attributes 165, 182, 200–4
'bordercolour' attribute 183
Borders
    around frames 113
    around graphics 42–3
    around images 165

 element 150, 177
Broadband connection 32
Browsers 2, 4, 7, 10, 127–8
Bullet types 190
Buttons 121–4

C

Capitalisation 15, 136
Cascading style sheets *see* CSS
Case-sensitivity *see* Capitalisation
'cellpadding' attribute 183
'cellspacing' attribute 183
CERN Laboratory 5
CGI 117–18, 155
CGI Directory 117

Chat rooms 117
Checkboxes 119, 121, 167
<cite> element 150
'class' attribute 152
Class selectors 62; see also Custom styles
'clear' attribute 204–5
'color' attribute 154, 205
Colours 36, 96–100, 149
    definition of 97–8
    in HTML 3.2 50–1
    see also 'bgcolor' attribute
'cols' attribute 160, 187
'colspan' attribute 184
Comment marks 60
Common Gateway Interface *see* CGI
Compression of files 95, 99, 101
Connection speeds 31–2
Controls 167
C++ language 117
CSS 46–7, 56–69, 180, 192
    custom styles 62–4, 143
    external stylesheets 64–9
    structural elements 58–61
    style rules 54–8
    syntax 194–6
    .css files 56, 62, 64–5, 88
CSS-P 71, 78
    for managing layout across a site 85–92
    style attributes in 79–81
Custom styles 62–4, 143
CuteFTP 134

D

Databases 117
Declarations for selectors 55–6
Degradation 47, 56, 84
Descriptions 173–4
  as displayed by search sites
    141–2
Dial-up connections 31–2
Directories 18, 32
Directory sites 139
Dithering 97–9
<div> tags and <div> boxes 71,
    78–85, 151, 153
Dots per inch 96
Download times 95, 136–7
Dreamweaver 2, 78, 103

E

e-commerce 117
Elements within documents 10,
    19–25
<embed> tag 131
Emphasis elements 20

F

'face' attribute 154
File names 15
File Transfer Protocol see FTP
Fireworks 2
Flash player 130
'float' attribute 205

Flow charts 29
Folders 18, 32
Font attributes 206–7
<font> element 153
Font size 52–3, 154
Fonts
  choice of 49–50
  preferred 154
<form> element 118, 155, 167
Formatting tags 45–8
Forms 117
  design of 124–5
<frame> element 157
'frame level' attribute 159
'frameborder' attribute 158–9
<frameset> element 159–60
Framesets 105–15
  nesting of 108–9, 159
FrontPage 78
FTP 5
FTP clients and servers 133–5

G

'Get' form of interaction 118
GIF 95, 99–100, 102
  interlaced 99–100
Gradients of colour 97
Graphic Interchange Format
    see GIF
Graphics 37–40, 94–100
  colour in 97
  hyperlinks for 42–3
Graphics cards 96

H

\<head\> element 19, 161
'Headings 1 to 6' 19, 160
'height' attribute 165, 183, 185,
    208
Helper applications 127–30
Hexadecimal values 98
HomeSite 2
Horizontal rules within text 162
HotDog Pro 2
Hotspots 102–3
\<hr\> element 162
'href' attribute 40, 65, 145
'hspace' attribute 166
.htm suffix 15
HTML 4–10, 16
    development of 45–6
    layout in 71
    specification 3.2 45, 47–54
    specification 4 46–7, 78; *see*
        also CSS
HTML editors 125, 133
\<html\> element 163
HTML tools 2, 102–3
HTTP 5
'http-equiv' attribute 173
Hyperlinks 40–3
Hypertext 5–6, 35
HyperText Markup Language
    see HTML
Hypertext reference attributes
    see 'href'

I

'id' attribute 152
Image element *see* \<img\>
Images 94–100
    colour in 97
Imagemaps 102–3
\<img\> element 37–40, 94, 164
Indenting of text 23, 147, 213
Indexed colour 99
Indexing of sites 140, 143–4
Inheritance, concept of 192–3
In-line elements 127, 192
Input controls 167
\<input\> element 119–20, 167
Intelligent agents 139
Interface elements, forms used
        as 117
Interlaced GIF 99–100
Internet, the, origin of 5
Internet Explorer (IE) 2, 4, 10,
        56–8, 113, 128
Italic text 20, 164

J

JPEG 95, 101–2
    progressive 102

K

Kerning 208
Keywords 140–2, 173–4

L

Layering of <div>s 81
Layout
  in CSS-P 85–92
  in HTML 71
  using tables 74, 78, 125
'letter-spacing' attribute 208–9
Line-height 209
Line-through style in text 212
Linking 35–40, 145, 149, 172
  to out-of-line elements
    128–31
Lists 25–6, 172, 175, 190
Live Audio 128
Local site folders 34
Lossy compression 101
Lycos 139

M

Macromedia 103, 130
Margins 166, 194, 209
Mark-up based languages 7–10
Matt's Script Archive 117–18
Measurement, units of 196
Menus, creation of 123–4
<meta> tags 140–2, 173
Method (of data submission
    from forms) 156
Monospaced fonts 124, 178
Mosaic 45
Multimedia 127, 129–30, 175
Multiple-choice questions 121,
    123

N

'name' attribute 145, 171, 173, 187
  assigned to a <frame> 157
Navigating a site 28
Nested framesets 108–9, 159
Netscape 113, 192
  Communicator 4, 127
  Navigator 45, 80, 84, 128
<noframes> element 113–15, 174
'noresize' attribute 158
'noshade' attribute 162
Notepad 1–2, 6, 12

O

<object> element 175
<option> element 176
Ordered lists 25, 175, 190
Out-of-line elements 127–9, 192,
    194
'overflow' attribute 209–10

P

Padding 183, 194, 210–11
Page properties 50
PageMill 78
Pages, creation of 12–15
Paintshop Pro 2
Paragraph (<p>) element 19,
    150, 177
Paragraph returns 12
Passwords 133
Pathnames 18, 33

PERL language 117
Photographs 97, 101–2
Photoshop 2
Pixels 2, 29, 95–6
Plain text 6
Planning a site 28–32
'pluginpage' attribute 131
Plug-ins 127–31, 175
Pop-up lists 123–4, 176, 178
Position attribute 211
'Post' form of interaction 118
<pre> tag 124, 178
Protocols 5
Publicising a site 139
Publishing a site 133
Python language 117

Q

Questionnaires 117

R

Radio buttons 119, 121–2, 167–8
Refreshing a document 173–4
'rel' attribute 65, 172
Relative links 33–4
'repeat-x' and 'repeat-y' 199
Reset buttons 122, 169
Resolution
   of graphics files 95
   of monitors 29
Rich Music Format 130
Robots 139–40

'rows' attribute 160, 188
'rowspan' attribute 185

S

Scripts 117–18
Scrolling 113, 123–4, 158
Search engines 139–40
Search sites 140–4
<select> element 123, 178
Selectors for stylesheets 55–6
Servers 5, 117–18
Shorthand 195
SimpleText 1–2, 6, 12
'size' attribute 154, 162, 170
   for images 94
Software requirements for
      creating a site 1–2
Sound files 127
Source code 9
Spaces in code 12
<span> element 179
Spiders 139–40
'src' attribute 158, 166, 171
<strong> tag 22–3, 180
Structural markup 16–18
Style 79–81, 146, 180
Stylesheets 46, 50, 53–5, 172
   external 64–9, 85, 89, 92
.subHead style 88
Submission to search sites
      143–4
Submit buttons 122, 168–70
Syntax 4, 56, 194–6

T

<table> element 181
Tables
  creation of 71–2
  used for layout 74, 78, 125
Tags 7–12, 143
'target' attribute 146
Targeting of links 109–12, 157
<td> element 184, 188
Template files 89
'text-align' attribute 212
'text' attribute 149
'text-decoration' attribute 212
Text editors 1–2, 6
Text fields 119, 167, 170
<textarea> element 119–20, 187
Tiling 53–4, 148
Timing see connection speeds;
  download times
Titles 19, 188
  for framesets 159
  for web pages 143
<tr> element 188
Transparent pixels 100
'type' attribute 167

U

Underlining 190, 212
Unix 15, 136
URLs 32–3
User agents 7; see also browsers
User names 133

V

'valign' attribute 186, 189
'vlink' attribute 150
'vspace' attribute 166

W

Web addresses 33; see also
  URLs
Web safe palette 97–8, 215
'width' attribute 163, 165, 183,
  185, 213
Wildcard values 160
Windows Explorer 134
Windows Media Player 128
WordWrap 12
World Wide Web, origin of 5–6
World Wide Web Consortium
  (W3C) 45, 50, 53, 78–9, 150,
  153–4, 161–2, 181
  HTML 3.2 specification 45,
  47–54
  HTML 4 specification 46–7,
  78
WYSIWIG 1–2, 78, 102, 125, 133

Y

Yahoo! 139

Z

Z-indexes 81–2, 21